The Spiritual TOP 50

THE SPIRITUAL TOP 50

wes moore

ISBN 978-1-4507-2886-7

Printed in the United States of America.

First Edition.

Cover by Chris Vestal.
Layout by Tiffany Dorrin.

To those who dare ask, “Why?”

The Spiritual
TOP 50

Table of Contents

1 **Foreword**

5 **Introduction**

Part 1: Evangelism Principles

9 *Ch. 1 | The Seven Laws of Evangelism*

19 *Ch. 2 | Relate: Befriending the Lost*

27 *Ch. 3 | Educate: Identifying Spiritual Background and Barriers*

41 *Ch. 4 | Answer: Overcoming Barriers With Answers*

47 *Ch. 5 | Present: Sharing the Gospel*

Part 2: Apologetics

71 *Ch. 6 | Apologetics: The Basics*

83 *Ch. 7 | The Seven Laws of Apologetics*

The Spiritual Top 50

93 *Ch. 8 | God Questions*

103 *Ch. 9 | Bible Questions*

113 *Ch. 10 | Jesus Questions*

123 *Ch. 11* | *Science Questions*
135 *Ch. 12* | *Truth Questions*
143 *Ch. 13* | *Church and Christianity Questions*
155 **Notes**
161 **Appendix 1: Recommended Resources**

Foreword

I still remember the first time I came across Christian apologetics. Having completely blanked when asked by a coworker why I believed the Bible was anything more than "just another old book," I began searching frantically to find the answer. That day, for the first time in more than twenty years of churched life, I came across the wonderful world of apologetics.

One reason our churches are failing today is because our people are unprepared for the questions they get from an unbelieving world. By God's grace, I eventually found the answers needed to restore my trust in what I had been taught, but for many others the questions and objections to their faith remain unanswered. Complacency and emotionalism dominate most American churches, and believers are left ill-equipped for the reality of intellectual spiritual warfare.

The book you hold in your hands is one man's effort to push back the tide of a church that values shallow faith.

Wes Moore has answered 50 of the most common questions and objections that Christians face today, and he has done it in a way that is accessible to the average believer.

We are unbelievably blessed in this day and age with a plethora of great minds that actively defend the faith in various intellectual arenas. As brilliant as many of the arguments put forth in lectures and debates are, one must wonder how easily they translate into everyday discussions between coworkers, friends, and family members.

What if we didn't just have a handful of great Christian thinkers that traveled around the country defending the faith? What if, instead, we also had an army of everyday believers who were equipped to answer the questions so many people are asking? How much more could be done across this nation, and even around the world, if average Christians like you and me personally responded to the intellectual obstacles people around us are facing?

That picture is the backdrop of this book. Wes has written a simple-to-use and easy-to-understand book for everyday Christians. He has taken the arguments from the university classroom, distilled them, and put them in a format that every believer can utilize.

But this book is not intended to be an end in itself. For what good is it to have the answers but never share them? To help you learn to share what you know, Wes has included several chapters on contemporary evangelism strategies from his book *Forcefully Advancing: The Last Hope for America and American Christianity*. This only adds to the value of *The Spiritual Top 50*.

Throughout this book, Wes' heart for reaching the lost shines brightly, and his desire for you to share in the awesome work of the Great Commission has produced one of the most unique and helpful books in the subject of Christian apologetics and outreach. Read it, learn it, and then go out and "destroy arguments, and every lofty opinion raised against the knowledge of God" (2 Corinthians 10:5).

Kyle Valaer
Vice President
Evidence America

Introduction

Wake up! There's no more time to stand on the sidelines. The game is on, and we're down...big time. Muster your courage, step onto the battlefield, and engage the enemy.

But wait. You'll need some new weapons if you're going to help us win. And that's what this book is all about.

The battle for human souls is more intense than ever. Our culture has changed; people are so skeptical today; they're raised to doubt the Bible and the cross, and they think you're just a legalistic hypocrite trying to sell them your "Jesus story."

So you can't just knock on their door and expect them to become a disciple in five minutes. You need a new plan, a better strategy. You need to engage them at a deeper level and labor with them over a longer period of time. You've also got to answer their questions and overcome their objections. If you can't dismantle the lies and false teachings that encompass their stony hearts, you'll likely walk away disappointed.

Enter *The Spiritual Top 50*. This book is designed not only to give you answers to fifty of the most common questions asked in the culture about God, the Bible, Jesus, science, truth, and the church, but also give you evangelism principles from *Forcefully Advancing*, a powerful new book designed to help you engage the lost in our twenty-first century culture.

The Spiritual Top 50 has two parts. Part 1 lays out the evangelism strategy you need to adopt to find success in witnessing in contemporary society. You'll learn the "Seven Laws of Evangelism," a compact set of foundational principles for effective evangelism, and the REAP process, a four-step process to engage the lost in your sphere of influence.

In Part 2 you'll learn not only answers to the top fifty spiritual questions, but also the "Seven Laws of Apologetics," a collection of guidelines to make you more effective as you use apologetics to impact the lost.

Now, turn the page and get to work! There are souls to win, and time is short.

Part 1:
Evangelism Principles

Chapter 1
The Seven Laws of Evangelism

Before I review the REAP process with you, I want to share some basic principles of evangelism, what I call the "Seven Laws of Evangelism." These are things you need to digest and understand before you can make any real difference in building the kingdom. Following is a list and brief description of each of the seven laws.

1. The Great Commission is your personal commission. This isn't somebody else's job. It's yours. While it is true that some are specifically gifted by the Spirit to be evangelists and pastors (Ephesians 4:11), it is also true that the New Testament pattern is that everybody shared the good news regardless of whether they thought themselves specially gifted or not.

You may remember the woman at the well from John 4. She met the Messiah and proceeded straight into town to tell others about him (John 4:39). And then there's the demon-possessed man, who, after being healed, wanted to stay with Jesus. But Jesus told him to "go home to your family and tell them how much the Lord has done for you" (Mark 5:20).

But the one that seals the deal comes from the book of Acts. In Acts 8:1 the Scripture says that "all except the apostles were scattered throughout Judea and Samaria" because of the persecution in Jerusalem. Make sure you notice that the apostles, the pastors and evangelists, were still in Jerusalem. Then the Scripture says, "*Those who had been scattered* preached the word everywhere they went" (8:4). The leaders of the church were in Jerusalem (the pastors and evangelists) and all those scattered (the regular people like you and me) spread the word.

2. Get your priorities straight. Let's face it—most of us are too busy to evangelize. Hurried, stressed, overburdened—these words describe us daily. We have no time to reach the lost, and time is what we need. So before anything else, we need to make time in our schedules to invest in the lost around us. How do we do this?

First, we'll need to cut some of our church activities; don't abandon your church, but ask yourself if the list of things you do there are really that important. Then we'll need to cut some kid stuff; make time for your children first, but ask yourself if they really need to be involved in sports, and dance, and piano, and art, and band all at the same time and year round. And then there's me stuff and work stuff. The core problem here is selfishness. Whether it's our drive to climb the corporate ladder or our "need" to play golf every Saturday or watch football all day Sunday, what little discretionary time we have is quickly chewed up by putting self first.

3. Integrity, integrity, integrity. The way we live—it's one of our greatest weaknesses when it comes to promoting truth to others. From the pastor who has an affair with his secretary, to the jerk at the office who happens to be a deacon, to the overbearing boss who can't miss his Monday night Bible study, Christians today cause more problems for the gospel than all the devil's demons put together. Here are a few areas we've got to improve.

Language. Many Christians lose their witness because of the way they talk. Instead of demonstrating a changed life, they act (and sound) like everybody else. Common curse words, harsh criticism, sexually suggestive talk—these are the besetting sins of many of our people. But it should not be so. Let me remind you that God requires his people to have clean, pure language (Ephesians 4:29).

Character. Character, as someone said, is what a person is in the dark. It's who you are on the inside, something no one can hide forever. And you can't fool an unbeliever; if your actions are not consistent with your profession, your witness will be ignored. To improve your witness in this area, make sure you are demonstrating a strong work ethic in the workplace, be sacrificially honest in all your dealings, and stay true to your convictions even when it costs you.

Transparency/Being Genuine: To what extent do people get what they see with you? Are you trustworthy, open, and real? To make sure you're not sending the wrong message in this area, resist the temptation to gossip, and be quick to admit your weaknesses and share your struggles with your lost friends.

Pornography. The word pornography comes from the Greek root porne, which means "to sell." Derivatives have similar meanings: porneuo means "to prostitute" and porneia means "prostitution."[1] According to one source, the word pornography dates to the mid-1800s and literally means "writing about harlots."[2]

The Lord Jesus Christ strictly forbids this type of lustful looking. "But I tell you," he declared sharply, "that anyone who looks at a woman lustfully has already committed adultery with her in his heart" (Matthew 5:28).

For help overcoming pornography, visit Focus on the Family's website and search for "pornography." The direct link is http://www.focusonthefamily.com/lifechallenges/love_and_sex/pornography.aspx.

How can we develop and maintain this type of integrity? Essentially it boils down to a close walk with Christ. Regular prayer, Bible study, and worship (among other things) are the backbone of strong Christian integrity.

4. If you're not taking risks, you're not evangelizing. Sacrifice, it seems, is the fuel in the engine of God. The Great Commission—the activity of promoting truth to others and forcefully advancing the kingdom of God—has, from its inception, exacted a heavy price from those who were willing to obey it. Here are some personal sacrifices it may require of you.

Relationships you hold dear and enjoy as they are. As you allow God to identify the lost in your circle of influence, he may burden you to risk a relationship that is important to you. A close family member, a coworker, a friend at school—all could be put on the altar for the sake of the kingdom. And, in the end, you may lose that relationship.

Financial welfare in terms of promotions and employment. The workplace is a ripe field for promoting truth; through work we can come into contact with many unsaved people and have access to them on a regular basis. In our society as it stands today, however, evangelizing at work can bring serious consequences. We can lose a promotion or even our job—but how else can we win them if we stay silent and comfortable?

Reputation and standing in your circle—the risk of abandonment and loneliness. We all want to be held in high regard by the people we know. But make no mistake, when you begin to promote Jesus, people will never think of you in the same way. Don't forget, a crucified Messiah is "foolishness to the Gentiles" (1 Corinthians 1:23) and today, a true Bible-believing Christian is even worse. You may find it a lonely place when you promote truth like Jesus.

The principle the Bible gives us is this: when faced with potential loss due to God's work, put the kingdom of God first and our well-being second. We must not allow ourselves to focus on the consequences for us, but on the good that God can and will do through our faithful risk-taking.

The Seven Laws of Evangelism
1. The Great Commission is your personal commission.
2. Get your priorities straight.
3. Integrity, integrity, integrity.
4. If you're not taking risks, you're not evangelizing.
5. Faith is a journey, not a lightning bolt.
6. Apologetics is not an option.
7. Expect success beyond your imagination.

5. Faith is a journey, not a lightning bolt. Contrary to popular opinion, most people in our culture don't come to faith in Christ in a flash, like a lightning bolt. Even those who appear to have been converted quickly have gone through some progression before making a commitment to Christ.

So, to be more effective in building God's kingdom, we need to adopt a broader view of conversion to reflect the process, or journey, people experience when entering it. To affect this, I have developed a three-part model I call Stages of Faith. Here are the three stages:

> *Stage 1: Gospel-hardened:*This type of person is, in terms of their progression, a long way from faith in Jesus. Skeptical, apathetic, antagonistic—these are the critics who don't trust what you say, and, though they may listen to you pleasantly enough, won't believe because they have already made up their minds. They may be atheists, agnostics, or idolaters. In any case, they're the tough nuts of outreach.
>
> *Stage 2: Gospel-open:* This person is closer to Jesus than the gospel-hardened. Willing to talk about Christianity and faith, they'll listen with an open mind to your case. They have a lot of questions and are willing to express them to you. Although they are not ready to make a life-commitment, their hearts are thawing to God and the Bible.
>
> *Stage 3: Gospel-ready:* Decision time—that's what you need to remember with the gospel-ready. They have learned about Christianity, may already understand much of the gospel, and are considering making a commitment to Christ. Having satisfied most of their questions, their hearts are open to the true message of

the Bible and its ramifications upon their lives.

Here are a few lessons to take from the Stages of Faith model:

- *As you talk to new people, learn to recognize where they are along this progression.* Ask yourself which of the three descriptions listed above fits your new friend best.
- *Because everybody is not at the same place in their faith process, you're not going to reap every time you engage someone.* So take the pressure off yourself. Labor with each person with the goal of moving them to the next stage and, in the process, preparing them for harvest in the future.
- *Finally, let this concept give you a longer-term view of promoting truth to others.* Relax and remind yourself that you're stepping into a process—sometimes a very long one—and the important thing is not that you do everything, but that you do your part and do it well.

6. Apologetics is not an option. Everywhere you turn today, the Devil promotes his lies about the Bible, Jesus, and true Christianity. Children are raised to doubt the Bible's reliability, the exclusive nature of Jesus, Noah's flood, the Garden of Eden, miracles, and nearly everything else the Bible teaches.

In this environment, to assume the average non-Christian has no issues that will keep him from being a sold-out, Bible-believing Jesus freak is absurd. Think about it like this: Why would you accept the Jesus of the Bible if you have rejected the Bible of Jesus? You wouldn't. And that's the point.

Amazingly, some people who teach evangelism skim over apologetics. And some people even think they can do evangelism without learning apologetics! They think if they just quote the Bible enough or share the message enough times, eventually the person will see the light. But they couldn't be more wrong!

To effectively engage the lost in our culture, we must stop seeing apologetics as a side issue. As those who see the Great Commission as our personal commission, we must also see apologetics as one of our most important tools and endeavor to learn more and more answers to faith questions over time.

Don't let that discourage you, however. Answering basic questions about spiritual matters doesn't require a PhD. Most of the lost people you'll be dealing with don't know that much. By learning simple answers you can overcome most of the objections that exist today.

7. Expect success beyond your imagination. It's easy to think no one will listen, that God has moved his work elsewhere and you're left to fend for yourself. You're willing to do the hard work, but deep inside you don't really believe anything remarkable will happen. That's where you're wrong.

A few years back, the Lord put it in my heart to go down to a bar not far from where I lived and witness to the patrons. I didn't want to do it; I'd spent a lot of time in those kinds of places before I was saved, and going back scared me to death. But the Lord wouldn't let up. I felt an almost physical pressure to go into that place.

When I walked in, the only guy sitting at the bar got up and walked out. "You sent me in here for a reason, Lord," I thought. "I'm going to talk to somebody." So I started talking to the bartender.

As it turned out, Debbie was a 44-year-old woman who'd

just found out she was pregnant by a guy who was now in prison. When I started talking to her, she just broke down. Though she was happy about the baby, her pregnancy brought to light all that had gone wrong in her life. She was overwhelmed, scared, and ready to seek God again.

A few days later, to my complete surprise, Debbie came by church on Wednesday night. And then she came on Sunday. Since then she has become a faithful disciple of Christ. She's out of the bar, taking college courses at the local community college (where she's an honor student), and is raising Rachel (that's her little girl) without the bad influences of her loser ex-boyfriend. And all because I walked into the bar that day.

That's what God will do with you if you'll remember this rule: Expect success beyond your imagination.

Up Next

Now that we've laid down some foundational principles, let's move on and establish practical steps to carry out the work of evangelism, the REAP process.

Chapter 2

Relate: Befriending the Lost

The REAP strategy is a four-step process to use as you evangelize the lost. The term "REAP" is an acrostic where every letter stands for a different step. Here is a listing and brief explanation of each step:

R – Relate. Here we initiate and develop our friendship with the lost person.

E – Educate. At this stage we educate ourselves about the spiritual background of our lost friend, and the barriers that are keeping them from fully committing their lives to Christ.

A – Answer. During this phase, we give our lost friend answers to their questions and objections.

P – Present. This is the final step. Here we present the gospel in a way that relates to our lost friend, but also includes its three biblical elements: repent, trust, and commit.

To be most effective in today's environment, you need to follow these steps in order. Of course, you can use these principles in quick, hit-and-run types of witnessing opportunities, but you'll make the most difference if you follow them in order in a longer-term evangelistic context.

In the chapters that follow, each of the REAP steps will be explained in more detail. In this chapter, the first step, Relate, will be discussed.

(For a comprehensive discussion of the REAP strategy, along with many other critical evangelism principles, read *Forcefully Advancing: The Last Hope for America and American Christianity*. For more information visit, www.evidenceamerica.org.)

Relate—Becoming a True Friend to the Lost

To build a real disciple in today's environment, it helps to be a true friend. God and faith are sacred, emotional, personal things to most people. Some have been so hurt by religious folk, some have terrible sins to hide, and others are just hardheaded and stubborn (and need to be told). But whatever the case, to go where you need to go and deal with the issues you need to deal with, you have to gain the trust that is only given to a genuine friend.

Becoming a Friend

You may be wondering exactly how to do this. Most Christians don't know a lot of lost people, and rarely spend time hanging out with them. So, let me give you some guidelines as you take this first step.

Reach out to whom?

So who should I reach out to? The key is to select anyone with whom you have ongoing contact. Places to look first are neighbors, friends, coworkers, schoolmates, dorm mates, customers, or family (immediate or extended). Bingo partners, bridge club members, the waitress at your favorite restaurant, that kid in math class, your son's little league coach, an old friend from high school—all of these are examples of opportunities we so often overlook. You don't have to go far to find more than you can handle.

How long will it take?

You may be thinking that making a friend will take a long time, but it doesn't have to. The process of earning trust and becoming a friend doesn't have to take years. Keep in mind, when I say friend, I don't mean that limited number of people you might consider your lifelong, true, dyed-in-the-wool, do-anything-for-you friends. These are truly rare. What I mean is someone who trusts you, likes you, and is more than a mere acquaintance. What you might call a "buddy" or "girlfriend."

The BUDDI System

It isn't always obvious how to initiate and develop a friendship with those around us. It can be intimidating, especially in the beginning. The BUDDI System, outlined below, lays out five helpful steps to developing friendships with the non-Christians around you. Begin putting these ideas into practice and you'll be a professional friend-maker in no time.

1. **B***efriend:* Make an initial acquaintance. This is sometimes the hardest part. However, it doesn't have to be difficult or complicated. Here are some ideas on how you can do this:

- Talk to a new friend in your high school biology class.
- When you check the mail, walk over and say hello to

your neighbor when he pulls in the driveway.

- Introduce yourself to a stranger in your college dorm.
- Stop that new guy from work in the hall and introduce yourself.
- When you see your neighbor cutting grass, walk over and say hi.
- Sit down beside someone new during lunch in the office break room.
- Take a walk down your street in the summer and see who's outside. Make eye contact and say hello.

Remember, you're just trying to introduce yourself. There's no religious discussion involved, no commitments of any type. You just want to chat, get to know them a little, and remember their name for later (and start praying for them).

I know you may be a little scared, but trust me. You're a friendly person. All you have to do is be yourself. Once you take the first step, you'll see how easy it really is.

2. **U***ncover:* Learn more about them over time. Once you've introduced yourself, you can start to uncover more about them as time goes by. This is important for two reasons: First, you want to be their friend; in order to do this, you need to become more acquainted with their lives. Second, later, when you are trying to engage them spiritually, you'll need this information to approach them in the right manner.

Here are three categories of information that will be helpful to you in your endeavor.

- *Personal:* You want to know about them personally. Here are a few things you can ask to help you get to know them. I'll phrase them as questions you can ask to help you see how to use them.

Where were you born? Were you raised there as well?
What's your favorite video game?
What do you like to do in your spare time?
Who's your favorite actor/actress/singer?
What is your favorite movie? TV show?
Are you a sports fan? Who do you like?
Where do you work?

- *Family:* You want to learn about their family. Here are a few specifics to talk about:

  Do you have brothers and sisters?
  Are you married? How long?
  Do you have children? Ages? Locations?
  Where do your parents live?

- *Spiritual background and barriers:* Eventually, you'll want to learn about their past experiences with religion, spirituality, and Christianity, as well as any barriers they have to faith in Jesus. We cover this topic in detail in the next chapter. For right now, just keep in mind that spiritual questions flow nicely right after family questions.

Asking good questions

Before we move on to the next step in the BUDDI System, let's discuss a critical part of becoming a friend: learning to ask good questions. Much of our anxiety related to getting to know new people comes from the fact that we don't always know what to say to a stranger.

Use the questions listed above when you first meet someone, and you'll find you're well on your way. In addition, you can use the following question-asking tools to keep the conversation moving.

- *Follow-the-answer principle.* After you ask a question, ask another question related to the answer to the previous question. Here's an example.

  Q: So, are you driving yet? A: Yeah, my dad just got me a car.
  Q: Cool. What kind of car? A: An old mustang.
  Q: What color is it? A: Red, but it really needs a new paint job.

- *Tell-me-about-that* principle. In this approach, you follow any answer with the statement, "Tell me about that" (or something similar). Here's an example.

  Q: Where are you from? A: Boston.
  Q: Tell me about Boston.
  Q: What took you to Boston? A: My dad was in the military.
  Q: Tell me about growing up in a military family.

- *How'd-you-like-that* principle. Here you follow any answer with the question, "How'd you like that?" (or something similar). Here's how it would work:

  Q: So, you picked a major yet? A: Yeah, chemistry.
  Q: How do you like it? A: It's okay. Just a lot of math.
  Q: And you don't like math? A: I do, but I didn't expect so much of it with a chemistry major.

3 . **D***ine:* There is no better way to open the doors of the heart than to share a meal with someone. In my experience, there is no better path to friendship—and ultimately meaningful spiritual interaction—than this.

With this step, you can either have your friend over to your home or apartment for dinner, or meet them at a restaurant and share a meal.

In either case, don't invite them until you've had a few chances to interact with them and learn something about them. If you have them over to your place, don't go overboard on dinner. You don't need to pull out the fine China and serve the roast beast. Keep it simple, and they will feel a lot more comfortable, and it will be easier to pull off.

As with other steps in the BUDDI system, spiritual conversation is not required. In fact, the first couple of occasions you want to be very careful here. Your first goal is to become their friend (their real friend). Spiritual things will come later. Relax, have fun, laugh a lot. No pressure on you or your guests.

4. **D***o:* Other than dinner, this is the best. When you find out what your friend likes to do, do it with them. Fishing, golfing, scrapbooking, Wii-ing (is that a word?); the field is wide open. Take the time and initiative to engage them in activities that are fun and interesting to them. After your friendship is solid, these events will be little mission trips for you.

BUDDI System Summary

Letter	*Name*	*Description*
B	Befriend	Make an acquaintance
U	Uncover	Learn about your friend
D	Dine	Have them over for dinner
D	Do	Do things they like
I	Improve	Help them when they need it

5. **I***mprove:* As you get to know more and more people and call more of them friends, trials inevitably will come up in their lives. Be available to help when they need you or when they're hurting. Give them a ride home after cheerleading practice; call them to check on their sick mother-in-law; take them a dish after their baby is born; host the baby shower; cut their grass when their mower is down; go to their brother's funeral; clean their side of the dorm when they're sick. If you're paying attention, the opportunities will be limitless.

Wrapping Up

Sometimes the hardest part about sharing your faith is getting to know new people who don't know Jesus. If you'll put into practice the simple things listed in this chapter, you'll quickly have a host of new friends that God will use you to influence. Now let's move on to the next step of our process, Educate, and learn how to understand the spiritual background and barriers of those we engage.

Chapter 3

Educate: Identifying Spiritual Background and Barriers

The devil is an expert marketer. Fifth Avenue's best are no match for him when it comes to promoting his product: lies. From television programs to the university and high school classroom, his message is everywhere. And what is it? Simple: the Bible isn't true. Whether it's "The Universe" on the History Channel promoting a false history of the world, or Dan Brown's novels questioning the trustworthiness of the gospels and integrity of the church, or Oprah Winfrey's New Age "god is in everyone" heresy, Christians and non-Christians alike are immersed in doubt-inspiring propaganda from every side.

In this environment, to assume the average non-Christian has no issues that will keep him from being a sold-out, Bible-believing Jesus freak is absurd. Remember: Why would you accept the Jesus of the Bible if you have rejected the Bible of Jesus?

So, after we have entered their lives as real friends, we must uncover anything hindering their full acceptance of our message. Before we begin, it is important to note that these two issues (spiritual background and barriers) are connected in most people; their religious background will shape not only their present beliefs but also their objections to Christianity. If a person is a second-generation agnostic, for example, they will likely view Christianity much differently than a person who was raised as a Mormon. But the views of both are driven by their religious background—and that's the point.

Although there is a definite connection, we'll deal with them separately in this chapter. So, let's begin with spiritual background.

Spiritual Background Defined

Spiritual background is defined as a person's past religious experiences and present religious beliefs. Everyone has a belief system they've formed over their lifetime to make sense of reality. This system contains convictions about spiritual matters, even if they don't believe in a supreme being or go to church on Sunday.

In order to lead them into the kingdom, we first need to understand their spiritual history and uncover their present beliefs. Here are some categories of information you'll want to uncover:

What is their spiritual history?

- Is (was) their family Christian, atheist, agnostic, Muslim, Hindu, New Age, or something else?
- Did they go to church growing up? If so, where and what kind?
- Are (were) their parents spiritual or church-going?
- Is (was) their parents' faith real? Is (was) it more than

just a Sunday morning thing?
- What kind of experience did they have in church?
- Have they attended church as an adult?

What are their present beliefs?

- About truth?
- About God?
- About Jesus?
- About the Bible?
- About heaven and hell?
- About life after death?

This information will be critical later when you attempt to get them past their issues to the cross of Christ. If you don't really understand where they're coming from, you'll struggle to give them an answer that connects with them. You can gather this information by using some of the questions listed later in the chapter.

Spiritual Barriers Defined

A spiritual barrier, in this context, is any objection that must be overcome before a person will commit fully to being a disciple of Jesus.

Here are some of the things you'll want to know:

- Of what are they skeptical? Religion, hypocrites, truth, the Bible, Jesus, God, or something else?
- Why are they skeptical? What are their specific issues?
- What are their questions about Christianity and its teachings?
- What are their misunderstandings about true Christianity and its teachings?
- What is keeping them from trusting the Bible and

believing the gospel?

Barriers are revealed when you start to ask about their spiritual background and present beliefs (previous section). In other words, when your friend starts talking about his background (religious or non-religious) and his present beliefs, at the same time he will be revealing his barriers to trusting Christ. All you have to do is listen carefully and compare his answers to the biblical truth you already know. That comparison will highlight for you key areas of concern and the objections or barriers you must overcome. Let me give you an example.

Let's say I'm talking to a person for the first time and I transition our conversation to spiritual things. As we move through the discussion (I'll walk you through how to do this in just a moment), I ask her about her background and present beliefs. Based on my simple questions, I learn the following:

- She was raised in a Methodist church.
- Her parents were not really religious people; they just went to church on Sunday.
- She left the church after entering college.
- She now attends a Universalist church (everybody is saved).
- She believes in the Great Entity (this is "god" to her).
- She doesn't believe in hell.
- She believes all religions are equally valid.
- She thinks the Bible is full of errors and contradictions.

You see, just by letting her talk about her religious past and present beliefs I have all I need to move on to the next step. I don't have to ask her directly why she doesn't believe in Jesus or the Bible, though I certainly can. She'll tell me on her own. Of course, this information may stir me to ask other questions, but the point is, I get both things I'm looking for with one set of questions.

So what kinds of questions can I ask?

Common Questions to Identify Spiritual Background and Barriers

Here are some questions you can use to uncover this information.

General Questions: These are questions you ask to get your friend talking about their past and beliefs. They make for good questions at the beginning of a spiritual discussion.

- Was your family a spiritual family?
- Is your family a spiritual family?
- Are you a spiritual person?
- What are your beliefs about God?
- Are you a "church-going" person?
- Tell me what you believe about heaven and hell.
- What are your views on religion?
- Tell me what you believe about Jesus.

Specific Questions: These are follow-up questions you can use to get more detailed information on important spiritual subjects. Use them to drill down in areas of concern or to clarify statements made to a general question (above).

God

- Do you believe in God?
- What is God to you?
- What kind of person is God?
- Can we know God?

- Do all religions lead to the same God?

Bible

- What do you think of the Bible?
- What is the Bible to you?
- Have you ever studied the Bible?
- Do you think the Bible is "God's Word"?
- Is the Bible true?

Jesus

- Who is Jesus to you?
- Why did Jesus die?
- Do you think Jesus was a real man?
- Do you think Jesus was God?

Salvation

- Do you believe in heaven and hell?
- How does a person get to heaven?
- What is "sin" to you?
- How does a person remove his/her sin?
- What is "salvation" to you?

Truth

- Can we know truth?
- How can we know truth?
- Is there absolute truth?
- Is truth relative?

Church

- Do you go to church now?
- Did you go to church when you were younger?
- What was your parents' faith like?
- What do you think of church?
- What kind of experiences have you had in the church?

- Why have you given up on church?

How do you know when you've got a problem? I can't give you an exact rule here. However, in general, when a person's beliefs reject a major biblical teaching, a red flag should go up. Major teachings include the existence of God, the nature of God (Triune, personal, knowable, creator, judge), the existence of truth, the reliability of Scripture, the deity of Jesus, the exclusivity of Jesus, the existence of heaven and hell, the reality of miracles, and salvation by faith in Christ alone. I'm sure you can think of others, but this is a broad-brush list to get you started.

Also, you can tell by the types of answers you get. If you get one or more of the following types of responses, you have some work to do before you can get them to the cross.

God

- I don't believe in God.
- I have my own view of God.
- God is the Great Entity.
- God is in all of us.
- God would not send anyone to hell.
- No one can understand the infinite.
- I don't know if there is a God or not.

Bible

- The Bible is a good book, but it was written by men.
- The Bible was good until it was distorted so badly.
- The Bible has been copied so many times; how can you trust it?
- I believe in evolution, not the Bible.
- I don't believe in talking serpents.

- I believe in science.
- The Bible is full of mythology.
- The Bible is full of contradictions and errors.

Jesus

- Jesus was a good person, but he wasn't God's Son.
- Jesus died to show us an example of sacrifice.
- We don't even know if Jesus ever lived.
- The church made Jesus divine, not Jesus.
- Jesus never claimed to be God.

Salvation

- I'm basically a good person, so I know I'll go to heaven.
- Sin is something we imagine, but it isn't real.
- If it's wrong to you, it's sin.
- There is no afterlife.
- God would not send anyone to hell.

Truth

- I don't think anyone can really know truth for sure.
- That may be true for you, but not for me.
- Truth is relative.
- How do you know you're right and I'm wrong?
- It doesn't matter what you believe as long as you love others.

Church

- I don't believe in organized religion.
- I think all religions are the same.
- All Christians are hypocrites.
- All religions lead to the same God.
- I am a Muslim (or any religion other than biblical Christianity).

You may be asking yourself what to answer first. People in our culture are so twisted in their thinking, they may reject virtually every major biblical teaching. How do I know where to go first? What should my priorities be? Good questions. But for right now, we just want to get the information out of them. We'll discuss what to do with it in the next chapter.

Pointers

Let me give you a few pointers where gathering this information is concerned. These are practical suggestions I've picked up over the years that may help you as you begin.

1. *Move through a progression in your questions.* In other words, don't just blurt out something like, "So, you a spiritual guy, Bob?" as soon as you meet someone. It is much more natural—and less in-your-face—to lead up to that question. Start with personal questions and then move to family questions. From family questions transition to spiritual questions.

Question Progression Funnel

2. *Pick a transition question and use it as often as you can.* You want to develop a pattern in your questions so you can get comfortable and come off as natural as possible. I like to use one of the first two from the General Questions listed above, like, "Was your family a spiritual family?" or, "Is your family a spiritual family?" It flows very well when you do it like that.

3. *Get the big picture before you think about answering.* Find out what your friend believes in at least the first four areas listed in the Specific Questions section (God, Bible, Jesus, Salvation) before you try to respond in any way. Don't jump to conclusions with partial information.

4. *Ask clarifying questions.* You'll be tempted from the outset to start answering their questions or arguing against their beliefs. Resist that temptation. Relax and make sure you really understand what they're saying. There will be a time for responding, but this isn't it. You are not in a fight. You are trying to understand so you can enlighten. Also, when you do answer, answer only specifics—you can't answer a generality.

5. *Gather this information in a conversation, not an interrogation.* You must practice having a conversation with your friend. You are not a highly paid attorney on a capital murder case. Ask questions and listen. Be interested. Smile. Ask more questions. Listen some more. Remember, you're just talking with a buddy or girlfriend.

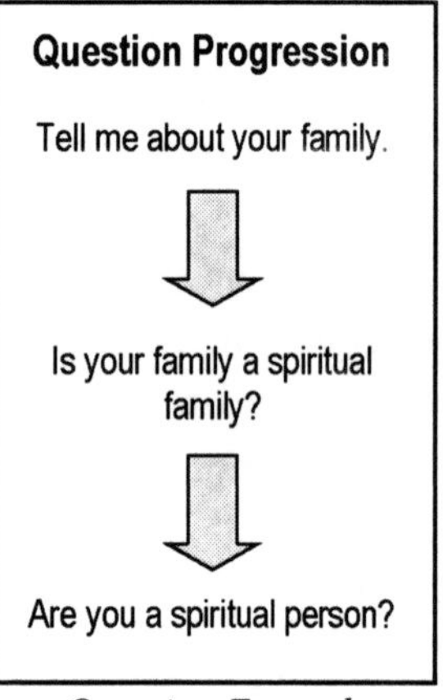

Question Example

6. *This conversation may happen in installments.* You may start your discussion at lunch break one day, get cut off, and finish it three weeks later. Be patient. God will arrange for another meeting. You're in this for the long run anyway, right?

What to Do When You Can't Do Anymore

You may be reading this, thinking, *Okay, I'm with you thus far. But I just can't go any further. I can be a friend, ask better questions, entertain, and maybe figure out why my friend won't believe. But I just can't take the next step of getting into a deep discussion about their issues or presenting the gospel. Should I just give up, or are there other options for me?*

Well, I have some good news for you: You're not alone. Many of us have this same struggle. Sometimes we feel like we don't have the right gifts or skills to engage the person at the next level. Other times, frankly, we're just too scared. Yet we continue to feel a responsibility and desire to be a part of God's redemptive plan for those around us. We want to do more.

So, first, know that it's all right to feel this way. You are not a disobedient disciple because you have this struggle. Don't feel inferior or be down on yourself; our Father knows the intent of your heart, and he is overjoyed with your desire to please him through obedience. Secondly, be encouraged because there is a lot you can still do. You are and can continue to be a critical player in God's purpose for those around you. Let me share a few things you can do from this point forward.

1. *Don't underestimate yourself.* You may think your sense of fear or inadequacy is a sign that you've reached the limits of your abilities or calling. While possible, this may not be the case. Feeling fear or inadequacy coupled with a desire to do something despite your fears can be a sign to step out of your comfort zone and grow. Your gifts may be hidden or simply need further development through experience. In my own case, early on when I thought about or tried to promote truth to others, I experienced a tremendous

amount of trepidation and found myself ill-equipped to deal with the questions and objections of others. But there was something inside me pushing me to engage others anyway. Over the years, I have learned how to do it better (which is what you are reading in this book) and have acquired, through a lot of hard work, many of the answers I need.

2. *Accomplish the plan up until this point.* Develop friendships with the lost around you, understand their spiritual background, and identify their barriers to faith—those things we have outlined thus far. You may wonder what you can or cannot do after these steps, but if you are to be used in any way, you must be engaged at this level. Remember, do these naturally; don't put pressure on yourself. Ask questions and listen to the answers. Make the friendship strong.

3. *Share resources to help address barriers and make the gospel presentation.* So, in this situation—where you don't think you can continue alone—the key to fulfilling the next two steps, the A and P of our acrostic, is to use the gifts of others to finish the process. You don't have to know all the answers, *just know the people who do*; you don't have to give an eloquent gospel presentation, *just put them in front of someone who can.* Here are a few different ways to do this:

a. *Get input from your Christian leaders.* Have a conversation with a wise Christian you trust about your friend, their background, and their issues. Get some ideas as to what to do next or how you should respond to a question or objection. Wise Christian leaders can recommend strategy, share stories of similar experiences with others, and send you to resources you never knew existed.

b. *Give them a book, article, CD, or DVD that addresses their issue.* This is a low-pressure way to start overcoming their objection. A couple of pointers here. One, make sure you ask them what media they prefer (do they read a lot, or do they prefer to watch something on video or listen on their iPod?). You want to get them the resource they are most likely to use. Two, review the resource yourself. You don't have to know it all; just be familiar with it in case you get a question or it leads to further conversation. Three, follow up on the resource. Don't call them the next day or anything, but make a note to follow up after a few weeks to see if they got anything out of it.

c. *Schedule an introduction to someone else.* When your relationship is strong enough, you can ask your friend to have lunch with you and another Christian who can help you deal with their concerns. Make sure the Christian you invite is good with people, aware of the sensitivities of the lost, and knowledgeable in the subject matter at hand. An enhancement to your relationship, a credit to Christ—this is what you want this person to be.

d. *Invite them to an appropriate event.* Group events can be a real plus here. At any one time, there may be several events in your area that would address your friend's issues. Whether they are answers about evolution, the basics of Christianity, or the gospel itself, you are likely to find helpful gatherings in close driving distance to which you can take your friend. A couple of recommendations here as well. Make sure the event fits the need. Don't take them to just any gathering; ensure it focuses on their interests. Also, don't take them to some high-powered evangelist unless that is the need at the time.

4. *Pray earnestly.* Nothing—no event, no resource, no other person—can do what prayer can do. No matter where you are in the process, never stop praying for real spiritual change in your friend, the success of your efforts to reach him or her, and wisdom to know what to do next.

5. *Keep the friendship alive and growing.* You may reach a stage where you are not sure what to do next. Or, your efforts to move the spiritual conversation along may meet some resistance or delay. Regardless of these things, keep the friendship alive. Continue reaching out in a non-spiritual way, strengthening the bonds for when God brings about the next step.

You may think you can't do much, but if you will step a bit out of your comfort zone, you can still make a big impact by following these simple guidelines. It isn't important who does the work, only that it gets done. Using your friendship as the foundation and your Christian brothers and sisters as your resources, you can complete your task and see your friend become a genuine, radical disciple.

The Next Step

Now that you understand some of their potential roadblocks, you can begin to address them. That's what the next chapter is all about. What is the most important issue to address? Where do I go for resources? What process should I follow? These questions and more will be covered next.

Chapter 4

Answer: Overcoming Barriers With Answers

So, at this point in our process we have asked a lot of questions and should have a good idea what our friend's issues really are. What next?

Well, first of all you need to decide which particular question or group of questions (sometimes you can distill them down to an underlying theme) to address. Prioritize them in your mind, either by importance theologically or importance to them. Obviously, whether or not the Bible has been corrupted by man is a more important issue than whether or not Moses actually wrote the book of Genesis. Furthermore, if the person brings up hypocrisy five times and Cain's wife only once, you may want to attack the hypocrisy issue first.

Another good rule is never get caught up with trivial matters; you want to major on the majors. Things like the trustworthiness and validity of Scripture, key gospel concepts like sin, judgment, and forgiveness; the deity, resurrection, and death of Jesus; and key elements of God's nature and character are where you should spend most of your time.

On a related note, don't feel like you have to answer every question. We'll talk about this more in just a moment, but what you really want to do is pick a few foundational issues, address them, and move to biblical truth.

Deciding Which Question to Answer
1. Prioritize by theological importance.
2. Prioritize by importance to them.
3. Major on the majors.
4. Don't try to answer every question.

You can also start by explaining the faults in their belief system first. For example, let's say your friend believes that evolution is true and, therefore, Christianity cannot be. Most of us would start by defending our faith—because we're offended by their unbelief—but our arguments will hit harder if we show some discipline and put our friend on his heels first. So you start by revealing the weaknesses of evolutionary theory—mutations and natural selection don't add information, dating methods are based on unprovable assumptions, the fossil record is incomplete (see Science questions in Part 2)—causing him to doubt his own beliefs and giving your arguments for Christianity more impact.

Once you've settled on the question you want to overcome, here's a simple process to work through to bring a solid answer.

1. *Understand the issue.* Don't jump to conclusions. Make sure you understand exactly what the person is saying before you start answering. I've wasted a lot of energy giving an

answer only to find out I didn't really understand the subtle nuance of the person's issue.

2. *Research the issue.* If you don't know the answer when the question comes up, be honest. Promise to bring back a good answer in the future (even if you think you know, it may be wise to take some time and get it exactly right). Then go research the answer. If you get stuck, reach out to a Christian friend or pastor for advice. Also, be sure to bathe the entire process in prayer. See Part 2 for answers to common questions and Appendix 1 for a list of additional resources.

3. *Share the information.* When you have the answer, organize it in your mind or write it down on paper so you can clearly communicate it. Think through any objections you may get and how you could respond. When you give the answer, if an issue comes up you can't answer, again, be honest. Go get the answer and come back; don't just start babbling. In the long-term, you'll have more credibility and you'll learn more yourself. Finally, be sure to leave them something to read so they can investigate it in more detail later.

You have several options when it comes time to give the answer to your friend. You can schedule another meeting with them and share it in person, or you could send them something (like an e-mail response, article, book, CD, or DVD) and then set a follow-up meeting to discuss what you sent.

Another option, if you think the discussion could be a lengthy one (this happens during the gospel hardened and gospel open stages in particular), agree with your friend to have an ongoing dialogue about the subject over e-mail.

Also, as I mentioned in the last chapter, you can invite them to an event that addresses their issue, if one is available.

4. *Drive to the Bible at a minimum, the cross if at all possible.* Remember: our goal is not to win an argument but to remove barriers so this person can believe. Therefore, I recommend you think through how you can transition from the question at hand to the authority and reliability of the Bible or to Jesus Christ and salvation directly. We don't want to get bogged down trying to answer every question and never getting to the core issue. Spend the time needed, obviously, but at some point drive them to the truth.

Here's an example. Let's say my friend has an issue with the errors in the copies of the New Testament. First, I need to give him the answer to his question. In short, although the New Testament documents aren't perfect, they are the most well-preserved documents in the world. (See Bible Questions in Part 2.)

Then, I'd say something like this, "So, you can see, though many people doubt the Bible because they think it isn't reliable, the reality is just the opposite. And this is what we'd expect if the Bible is what it claims to be—inspired and preserved by God. Maybe there's something to this Bible thing after all?"

5. *Plan the next step.* After the meeting, spend some time thinking through how you can engage the person again in the future to lead them even further down the road to genuine faith. Ask yourself, "Now that we've dealt with that issue, what is the logical next step in our discussion?"

The Process for Giving and Answer
1. Understand the issue.
2. Research the issue.
3. Share the information.
4. Drive to the Bible or the cross.
5. Plan the next step.

Conclusion

Giving answers is an essential part of expanding the kingdom of God. By understanding the issues of our friends, researching answers, and presenting truth in a compelling and loving way, with the Spirit's help we can overcome any barrier and see true transformation in those around us.

Now for the final leg of our strategy, the *P* of our acrostic, Present, sharing the gospel in a relevant and impactful way.

Chapter 5

Present: Sharing the Gospel

The word *gospel* means "good news" or "good message." Something new that is good or something new that brings good—this is what the gospel is. Jesus, of course, is at the center of the good news of the Bible.

You can look at the biblical good news as having three parts. First, there are *the benefits*. These are the good things that come our way through Jesus. The New Testament gives us many benefits that result from his coming into our world. The promise of deliverance from struggle, escape from the wrath of God, spiritual light and wisdom, and entry into the paradise of God are but a few examples of the positive impact of Christ's life.

Gospel Funnel

Then there is *the root cause.* The root cause is what Jesus did to bring about the good results mentioned above. Whereas the benefits are many and varied, the root cause is more concise and focused, and ultimately can be summarized in just two words: *the cross.*

Finally, there is *the activating action.* This is the action a person must take when they hear the gospel in order to make its benefits personally applicable. It's what I must do to be saved and have all of the gospel's benefits applied to me. Like the root cause, this aspect of the gospel is succinct and can be boiled down to just one word: *believe.*

When we share the gospel, we should be sharing all three elements: the benefits, the root cause, and the activating action. Equipping you to do this is what this chapter is all about. With this in mind, let me give you four goals for the pages that follow:

1. Give an overview of four benefits of the gospel.
2. Articulate the root cause of these benefits.
3. Explain the action a person must take for the gospel to apply to them.
4. Share how to ask a friend to believe and what to do if they don't.

Gospel Benefits

In the following paragraphs, I'll list and explain four benefits of the gospel. You should use these options as a tool bag as you evangelize. When the time is right to present the gospel message, pick one that applies to your friend's specific circumstances and share it with them. You know your friend well by now, and—with the Spirit's help—you can laser in on the portion of the gospel that will impact them most.

The first two benefits are specific and will apply only in certain situations. The last two, however, are universal as they apply to everyone at all times. Familiarize yourself with these and refer back to them later as you interact with different people.

Jesus, deliverer from trial and struggle

The down, the struggling, the hurting—these types of people were the Savior's favorite target. It seems those who were most open to his message were those who were most impacted by the cruel turns of life; and it is no different today. Trials have a way of breaking our arrogance and revealing our frailty and need. If you become a genuine friend to the lost around you, you will absolutely, positively see them go through a trial. And when you do, this may be the best benefit to share.

A God who cares

There are two ways to approach sharing the good news when your friend is in a trial. First, *you can introduce God as someone who cares.* You and I may have a hard time understanding this, but there are a growing number of people who don't think of God as a personal being who cares for them and desires to help. So, even though it may not seem like a lot, you can move someone along their path to salvation by simply pointing out that God is interested in their lives and cares for them.

I have a friend in Moldova (near Ukraine in the former Soviet Union) named Eugene. A wonderful Christian man, Eugene organizes outreach efforts for Campus Crusade for Christ in that country. When he tells the story of his conversion, he doesn't begin with Jesus, but with God. He says he found himself in need and for some reason prayed to God for help, and God answered his prayer; so, he prayed again, and again God answered. This happened over and over and eventually softened his heart to receive the gospel of Christ when he heard it.

Jesus who delivers

So, you can introduce your friend to a God who cares, or you can be more specific and *introduce them to Jesus Christ, who promises ultimately to bring about a permanent change in their desperate circumstances.* In this case, you go one step further and set forth Jesus, God in human form, as the one who promises to deliver them completely from what troubles them.

Jesus often presented himself as the supreme answer to the ailments of this age. Setting forth this benefit to your friends simply means telling them what he promises to do for them in the future. Before we list specific examples, however, let me say a few things about Christ's promises where trials are concerned:

1. It is very important to remember that complete deliverance is promised *only* in the eternal state, not in the here-and-now. This is the promise we can make confidently and without reservation. The examples of immediate deliverance are meant *to point to* the reality of full healing in the eternal state.

2. Though miraculous deliverances are possible today, they are not promised in every case and are rare. Hence, do not promise someone a miracle as a solution to their situation.

3. Trials are God's instruments for good and are not always removed even when we trust in him. Therefore, do not

promise that God will take the trial away, but that he will a) give strength to endure it, b) give wisdom to understand it, c) bring good from it, and d) bring it to an end at the right time.

Five troubles Jesus has promised to end

Here are five examples of troubles from which Jesus has promised ultimate deliverance. The first four come from Jesus' proclamation in Luke 4:18, and the last is from his promise in John 11:25–26.

1. *Deliverance from earthly poverty to kingdom riches.* "The Spirit of the Lord ... has anointed me ... to preach good news to the poor." The good news for the poor is that God's riches will be theirs because of Christ. "Blessed are you who are poor, for yours is the kingdom of God," announced Jesus in Luke 6:20. In other words, Jesus came to act on behalf of the poor so they could call the kingdom of God their own, presently as a promised possession and at the end of the age as a physical reality. So, though stricken with poverty now, they can, by believing in him, call all that God has their own.

When God leads you to someone struggling in this way, share this great benefit with them. You might say, "Sally, I know you and George are struggling financially, trying to make ends meet with so little. And I know it seems like there is no hope you'll ever get out of this hole. But there is a person who has promised one day to give you the greatest riches ever. Jesus said he would give God's riches to all who trust in him."

2. *Delivery from enslavement to freedom.* "He has sent me to proclaim freedom for the prisoners." Enslaved—it is a word that describes the human predicament perhaps better

than any other. Although many endure the bonds of physical prisons, many more bear the shackles of spiritual ones. Christ is promising eventual autonomy from all manner of enslavement, whether by people or spiritual powers or sin. This freedom, which begins at faith in him, will find its consummation in the eternal state. Make sure your friends with addictions (like pornography, alcohol, or drugs), those in abusive marriages, or those bound by prostitution—to name a few—encounter this liberating message.

You could use these words, "Susan, there is someone who has promised to bring an end to this abuse…forever. Not only will he help you now but also take you to a place where abusive relationships no longer exist. That person is Jesus Christ."

3. *Delivery from blindness to sight.* "He has sent me for recovery of sight for the blind." Of course Jesus did literally heal the blind on the spot on several occasions, but it is hard to overlook the larger spiritual significance of his words here. Physical blindness, as heartbreaking as it is, is no match for the tragedy of spiritual blindness; physical blindness, after all, cannot estrange one from the life of God, deny him authentic wisdom for living, or damn him to hell. With his coming, Jesus the Messiah promised to all genuine spiritual sight and all of its rich benefits.

Those who worship a false god, those who need wisdom for life (kids, marriage, work, and relationships), those who are bound by a cult, and those who are asking questions—don't withhold the blessing of light from those who need it most. Try a statement like this, "Don, it looks like you need someone to show you which way to go. You've tried your ways, but they've only made things worse. You've tried the advice of friends, yet they haven't helped. But there is a man who promises to give us real wisdom if we ask. How would you like that? His name is Jesus Christ."

4. *Delivery from abuse to love.* "He has sent me to release the oppressed." To those so blessed to cross his path, Jesus offered love, tenderness, and empathy, while others, only cruelty, abuse, and exploitation. His appearance in time was intended to bring relief to those suffering such circumstances and apply the healing only the Father's love could convey.

As you know, every day in our world children are abused, wives deserted, employees exploited; people are oppressed because of their color, age, sex, income, sexual orientation, and every other reason you can imagine. Consequently, countless souls for whom Christ died see no value in themselves and no love in their future. As you encounter those with such need, don't hesitate to bring them to the loving Jesus.

"Phil," you might say, "in your life, you haven't seen a lot of real love, not from your father, not from your mother, not even from your friends. I know how heartbroken you must feel. But there is someone who has always loved you and who wants to show you more love. His name is Jesus Christ."

5. *Delivery from the grave to the second life.* "He who believes in me will live, even though he dies; and whoever lives and believes in me will never die." In this situation as recounted by John, Jesus was faced with a family who had lost a loved one, Lazarus. In the exchange with Lazarus's sister Martha, Jesus dispenses one of the most profound benefits of his gospel: resurrection from the dead. In so doing, he gave incredible comfort to all who will die—that's all of us—or

have lost loved ones to the strong arms of death. There is another life, a second life, to follow; death is not the end of the story. Reach out with this message to those around you who are face-to-face with sickness and death.

You could approach your friend like this, "Bobby, I know you lost your brother a few weeks ago, and I know what an effect it's had on you. At our age, we aren't too far behind; you're probably thinking about your own mortality more these days too. But did you know there is a person who promises a second life to us, a life after death? Jesus Christ said, 'Whoever lives and believes in me will never die.'"

Jesus, the giver of meaning and purpose

No Christ, no meaning. No Christ, no purpose. That's the hard truth about this life. Without Yeshua, there is no God to love our souls, no afterlife to revive our bodies, no forgiveness to ease our consciences, and no purpose to gather our passions—only loneliness, only darkness, only death. This life is it, like it or not.

People know this whether they can articulate it as such or not. I was talking with a man named Al once at a local home improvement center. He shared with me how at his age (he was in his late fifties) most of his relatives and family were dying off; the only one left was his father, who was eighty-five. When I asked him if he was a religious person, he told me this: "No, I'm not a religious person. I'm no better than a cockroach crawling across the floor. When I die, 'poof,' that will be it for me."

Yes, without Messiah, Al is dead on—we're all simply cockroaches doomed to a life of pointless labor, one day simply to vanish into the dust. But because Jesus has indeed come, because Jesus has indeed done his magnificent works, because Jesus has indeed made his tremendous promises, there is reason to live.

Try words like these, "Taylor, I can tell you're a person who wants their life to mean something. And lately it seems you're looking for a higher purpose and meaning to life. There is a person who can give you the type of meaning you're looking for. His name is Jesus Christ."

Jesus, the means to the paradise of God

This example is similar to a previous gospel benefit, Jesus as the deliverer "from the grave to the second life." However, I want to include this section because its truth—the paradise of heaven, biblical eternal life—provides a different and important motivation for the lost.

Perhaps the pinnacle of gospel benefits, and the one that incorporates most others, is the promised blessing to all believers of a "paradise of God" (Revelation 2:7). In every way the photo negative of our present world, this is a paradise where no one will die again or ever feel sadness; even the threat of harm or fear will not exist. Human beings will be given new abilities to experience and enjoy life as never before; we will know and interact with God as we cannot now imagine; and the Creator will lavish his kindness on us without end. Those we love who have died believing we will meet again, even our infant children, and this experience, called eternal life, will continue into infinity.

Share this with those who are tired of this world and long for a better place after death. You can say it like this, "Ben, I know you're struggling with the harshness of this life. You've seen a lot of death and suffering in your time, and it's getting you down. You wish there was something more than this down the road. Well, what if I told you there was? What if I told you there was a 'paradise of God' out there? Would you like to know the way?"

Jesus, the escape from the fires of hell

Hell. Don't be afraid to talk about it. Jesus did. In fact, he talked about it more than he talked about heaven. One writer comments, " ... the knowledge of hell comes almost exclusively from the teachings of Christ, who spoke emphatically on the subject on a number of occasions."[3] Some people cannot be persuaded by the positive benefits of Christ's gospel, many of which we have discussed in this chapter; so we must be willing to take them down a more difficult and dark path: the fearful reality of hell.

Hell is the place where God justly punishes those who have no covering for their sin. It is called "the fiery furnace" (Matthew 13:42), "the darkness" (Matthew 8:12), "the fire of hell" (Matthew 18:8–9), and is said to be far worse than death itself (Matthew 10:28).[4] According to the apostle Paul, it's a place where God's wrath is released without reservation, resulting in "trouble and distress for every human being who does evil" (Romans 2:8–9)—all of us, unfortunately. Without question, it is both a very real place and a very awful place, and, according to the Bible, a place to which all humanity is destined without Christ to rescue them. To quote Paul again, Jesus is the one "who rescues us from the coming wrath" (1 Thessalonians 1:10).

Therefore, as God leads you in interactions with the lost, make use of this benefit of the gospel without fear or hesitation. It is a part of God's Word and Christ's teaching, and, therefore, an invaluable tool in fulfilling our commission to make new disciples. "Shane," you could say, "I know you think you're young and invincible. You usually don't think about the future that much. But have you given any thought to what will happen to you after death? The Bible says there's a heaven and a hell. Hell is a real place [describe from above]. What if that's where you'll go when you die? Would you like to know how to escape that possibility?"

Cut-to-the-Chase Question

There may be occasions when you don't have the time to ferret out the specific benefits that apply to your friend. You might just want to cut to the chase and focus on the core gospel message. If so, there's a helpful question you can ask to focus in on a person's standing before God. It goes something like this: "If you died today and stood before God and he asked you, 'Why should I allow you into heaven?' what would you say?"

How can I be right with God? This is the question your friend is forced to consider. You'll get a variety of answers to this query, but most of the time people will say something like this, "I'm a good person. I've tried to help others, and I haven't murdered or raped anybody."

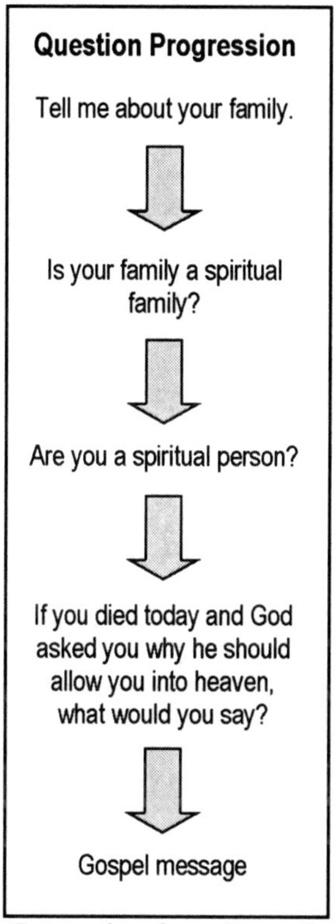

Question Progression

Tell me about your family.

↓

Is your family a spiritual family?

↓

Are you a spiritual person?

↓

If you died today and God asked you why he should allow you into heaven, what would you say?

↓

Gospel message

Cut-to-the-chase Example

Most people think they're good enough to make it on their own. But, as we know, nobody is. From here, you go directly to the root cause and activating action. You could say something like, "Yes, Jeff, it's good that you're trying to live a good life. But what if that isn't good enough? Did you know the Bible says that no one can be right with God by doing good?" [Then walk through the root cause and activating action.]

The Benefits Are Complete

Up to this point I've outlined four good results of the gospel that you can share with your friends as applicable to them. If you have followed the REAP steps up to this point, the benefit you should apply will come fairly easily. But no matter which one you choose to share with your friend, you also need to tell them how this great benefit came about. What is the root cause of this wonderful promise or blessing? That's what we'll talk about next.

The Root Cause

Imagine all of the benefits of the gospel as the upper portion of a funnel; these benefits flow into the spout, the narrow section of the funnel, which in our case consists of the root cause and activating action. Now, since we've discussed the benefits at length, let's discuss the items in the spout, starting with the root cause of gospel blessings.

As indicated earlier, the root cause of the innumerable benefits of the gospel is the cross of Jesus Christ. Ultimately, mankind suffers from a broken relationship with their Creator. Instead of having full access to his life, power, and blessings (which bring joy, peace, and hope), we have been banished from him, separated by an immense barrier—our immorality.

It is God's nature to hate and reject sin, anything that is contrary to his moral character. It is an irreversible, permanent part of who he is. Therefore, it is impossible for him to accept anything but complete and perfect morality in his creatures. This doesn't mean he's unfair or arbitrary, however; it means he's holy, pure, and separate in his perfections as a moral being. In order for us to come back into his favor and receive the great benefits of knowing him, the roadblock of our immorality must be overcome.

Another way to look at this roadblock is as a personal debt. Whenever we sin against someone, we incur a debt to them. If you've ever heard a criminal say, "I've paid my debt to society," you're familiar with this concept. What the criminal is acknowledging in this statement is that he has wronged society (by sinning against it) and, therefore, has incurred a debt to that society. In order for him to be "right" with society again, he must pay his debt. Prison is one way to do that. Some debts are so great, however, they're called "capital" crimes and require the person's life as payment.

In the same way, when we wrong God through sin, we too incur a debt; that debt becomes a barrier between us. Unlike crimes against people or society, however, *all crimes against God are capital crimes* and demand the life of the criminal as payment. The point? In God's system, *we're all on death row.* For our roadblock to be removed and our debt erased, God must act on our behalf. We cannot do it ourselves—it is impossible for us. So God, who loves us unconditionally, has set a plan in motion to make things right again. This is where Jesus Christ and the cross come in.

In the end, what Jesus has done is healed the relationship between us and God, putting God back on our side; he has paid our enormous debt so we don't have to suffer our terrible punishment. God, then—who is all the blessing, power, and life we need—is again fully engaged on our behalf to bring life to completion in perfect happiness. God's lone instrument for this task? The cross.

To put it in personal terms, Jesus Christ lived the life I could not live—without immorality—to die the death I dared not die—the crucifixion—to pay the debt I shall myself never remove—my sin. On the cross, Jesus willingly gave up his life as a payment for me so God's justice could be satisfied and his love and kindness flow freely to me again. God accepted Jesus as my substitute and confirmed it by resurrecting him from the dead, something only God himself could do.

One of the best illustrations I've ever heard to describe what happens at the cross is that of a judge and a capital murder case. A man had been accused of a crime so horrific that, if found guilty, the punishment would be execution. The evidence was so overwhelming, the judge had no choice; after giving his verdict, he issued the sentence: death.

The irony of the story, and the real tie to the gospel, is that the man who committed this crime *was the judge's son*. You can imagine the pain and anguish of this judge as he sentenced his own child to death. Though he knew his son was guilty and though he was satisfied that justice had been served, he mourned beyond words what he had been forced to do. What could he do now? His love only gave him one option. So, after the gavel fell, he stood up, took off his robe, and died in his son's place. "For God so loved the world that he gave his one and only son…" (John 3:16).

This is the picture painted for us in the Bible. God has been forced to judge all mankind guilty and sentence them to death for their crimes. But his love is so great, he takes off his robe and dies in their place in the person of Jesus of Nazareth. And now, far from standing over them, his finger wagging, he sends his word out to all, begging them to receive his forgiveness and deliverance.

Don't hesitate to share this powerful illustration with your friends.

Before we move on, let's summarize the elements of the root cause of gospel benefits:

- We have a broken relationship with God caused by our immorality.
- We owe a debt to God for our sin that we cannot repay.
- God has acted on our behalf through Jesus Christ.
- Jesus Christ has:
  - Lived the life we could not live, without immorality.
  - Died to remove the barrier between us and God by paying our debt.

The Activating Action

Having shared the benefits of the life of Jesus and articulated the root cause of his benefits, it's now time to explain the *activating action*, the way in which we make the gospel benefits apply to us personally. The word that characterizes this action best is *believe.*

Regardless of the particular benefit you seek, the way you make the gospel message apply to you is to believe, or trust, the content of the message. More than simply accepting certain facts as true, believing in Christ is also putting trust in those facts, relying on them at risk to yourself. When we believe the gospel, we trust that Jesus did as the Scriptures say—that he lived for us, that he died to remove the barrier between us and God, and that he rose again after three days to confirm his work.

Furthermore, by definition, we stop relying on what we had trusted in before. No longer believing we are good enough to earn God's favor or that our false gods can save us, we forgo any other means of being right with God or of entering into his paradise, transferring our trust completely to Christ.

As we now understand the horrible impact of our sin on our relationship with God, we repent, or mentally turn from our sin, and seek God's forgiveness. Believing also means I am willing to commit my life to God's service moving forward; inasmuch as Christ died for me, I now owe him my life. This is what it means to believe in him. And when we do, all the good God has accomplished through him courses our way irrevocably.

When we make this conscious choice, many things happen in a domino effect. We are instantly forgiven, and our debt is erased. We are adopted by God as his true child. Our names are written in God's book of salvation (called the Lamb's Book of Life), and we instantly become heirs of all his promises and future blessings. Moreover, God begins to work in us to change us into the pattern of his character. He gives us hope and confidence in the future, and he begins to use us to bring about good in the world.

Now, let me summarize the elements of the activating action:

- To be saved, we must believe, or trust, the content of the gospel.
- Trusting means we don't just accept certain facts, but trust in them at risk to ourselves.

- We trust that Jesus did as the Scriptures say.
- We must stop trusting that we are good enough or that any idol can save us.

- We repent of our sin.
- Since Christ died for us, we willingly commit to his service.

Asking Them to Believe

So you've shared the three parts of the good message. Now you need to ask them to believe. How do you do this? Let me lay out a brief process for you. But first, a few preliminary observations.

Remember that you are not responsible for their answer; God is. Ultimately it is God who brings men and women to faith, not me and you (Matthew 11:25–27, John 12:32, Ephesians 2:8–9). Furthermore, you don't need to apply pressure yourself; the message and the Spirit apply all the pressure needed John 16:7–11).

Also, before you do any asking, make sure your friend understands what you have told them. You can simply ask a question like, "Do you understand what I'm saying?" If they don't understand completely, don't move to the next step until they do. When you're sure they understand, ask them to believe. It is as simple as saying, "Do you believe Christ can do this for you?" or, "Do you want Christ to do this for you?" or, "Do you want to trust Christ?"

When they have expressed a desire to believe in Jesus, tell them how to formally ask God to save them through prayer. You can pray with them, or, if they seem uncomfortable, tell them what to pray in private. Here are the essential elements of the prayer: a) I want to be delivered, b) I believe Jesus died to deliver me, pay for my immorality, and to make me right with God, c) I repent of my sin, and

d) I give my life to Christ from this point forward.

Example conversation

Here's an example of how a conversation might go. First, I'll use one of the four benefits of the gospel, and then I'll use the cut-to-the-chase question, both from earlier in the chapter.

Gospel Benefit: Meaning and Purpose

Mark: "Well, I believe there's some kind of higher power out there, but I don't know that we can know anything about him."

I continue to ask Mark questions about what he believes and over time give him answers. During this time I discover that Mark is looking for meaning in his life. He's become disenchanted with what he's been told in the world. All their promises are empty, and he wants more from life.

Wes: "Mark, as we've talked over the past few months, I've sensed in you a desire for a greater meaning to your life. Am I on track?"

Mark: "I guess you are. You know I'm almost forty now, and I'm tired of the rat race. There's got to be more to life than this."

Wes: "I know what you mean. I had this same experience a number of years ago. Did you know there's someone who can give you the meaning you're looking for? His name is Jesus Christ."

From here I tell him about the meaning and purpose Jesus gives and what he has done in my own life. When I've explained it to him, I move on to the root cause and activating action.

Cut-to-the-Chase Question

Mark: "Well, I believe there's some kind of higher power out there, but I don't know that we can know anything about him."

In this example, I have a couple of options. First, I could ask him clarifying questions about what he believes, give him answers, and then use the cut-to-the chase question. In this case, I don't worry so much about which benefit I use, just go straight to the gospel. Or, I could leave off the additional belief questions and go straight to the cut-to-the chase question. Either way, here's what I'd say when I got to the question.

Wes: "Mark, let me ask you a spiritual question. If you died right now and stood before God, and he asked you, 'Why should I let you into heaven?' what would you say?"

Mark: "I guess I'd say that I'm a good person. I try to treat people as I would want to be treated. I try to do good. No, I'm not perfect, but I'm not as bad as some people."

Wes: "Yes, I know. Compared to other people, you haven't committed any great crimes. And it's good that you try to treat others right. But what if you're wrong? What if that isn't good enough? Did you know the Bible says that not even the best person on earth is good enough to be right with God?"

From here I move on to the root cause and activating action.

What if they don't believe?

What if they don't want to believe? What do I do then? First, find out exactly what they don't believe. Ask a question like, "What exactly do you not believe?" or, "Why do you not believe?" Listen carefully to their response, and ask clarifying questions if necessary; make sure you understand their specific issues clearly. Then proceed to address their issues. You may need to clear up misunderstandings, overcome existing or new barriers, or clarify previous points. In any case, deal with the issues, summarize the gospel, and ask them again to believe.

What if they still won't believe? As before, don't get mad. End the conversation on a friendly note and leave the door open for future discussion. You never want to make it impossible for you to talk to them again later because of something you said in anger or frustration. Continue developing your friendship outside of spiritual things, and keep praying for God's activity in their lives and guidance for you in terms of what to do next.

It may be time to move on

In the end, if they don't want to believe, your relationship may change. You've laid it on the line with them, and they may react in a negative way. Don't forget, there is something inside all of us that hates God and resists Christ. You may be the object of this disdain after you've spoken so boldly for him.

Keep working on them. Be friendly, pray for them, and look for future open doors, but if you sense their attitude has changed toward you, this may be an indication that your work with this person has come to an end. Your love for them will not change (your friendship was not fake), but in terms of the time you have to focus on them for the sake of the gospel, you'll be forced to curtail it. Free your conscience to move on to a new friend and focus your energy there.

But don't be discouraged. Your boldness, your courage, and your words have made an impact on their life. Have faith in God; he will bring fruit from your efforts in ways you cannot predict. Feel good about what you've done. You've just walked in the shoes of Jesus.

Conclusion

The gospel is a world-changing message. Its three-parts—benefits, root cause, and activating action—when presented at the right time and in the power of the Spirit can radically alter the life of our friends, schoolmates, neighbors, and coworkers. As the Spirit leads you, present the benefits of the gospel with rich variation, explain the power of the cross, and detail how your friend can make those alluring benefits their own.

Now that we've laid out some basic evangelism principles, let's change gears for Part 2 and talk about apologetics.

Part 2:
Apologetics

Chapter 6
Apologetics: The Basics

I can still remember the '84 starting lineup of the Atlanta Braves, my favorite baseball team growing up. There was Chris Chambliss at first, Glenn Hubbard (he was a short guy with a beard) at second, and Rafael Ramirez at short. Bob Horner played the hot corner, and Bruce Benedict caught. In the outfield you had Claudell Washington (a lefty with a smooth swing) and Gerald Perry in right (actually, I forgot about Gerald, so I had to look him up). And then there was *the man, my man*, Dale Murphy. Boy, how I loved that guy.

Born to be a baseball player, Murph—that's what they called him back then—played center, ran like the wind, and hit homers like rockets. I remember one in particular, a zinger over the right field wall. From the instant it left his bat, it couldn't have gone higher than twenty feet all the way out. That thing was a missile!

Murph was my baseball hero. Yet there is one big disappointment for me where he is concerned: he's not in the Hall of Fame. And I don't like that...at all. Let me tell you why. First, his stats for that time period were absolutely stellar. He led the National League twice in homeruns and RBIs (that's runs-batted-in for those of you who live on Mars); he was only the sixth player ever to have thirty homeruns and thirty stolen bases in the same season. Moreover, he was the only player ever to have a .300 batting average, hit thirty homeruns, drive in 120 runners, score 130 runs himself, and steal thirty bases in the same season (1983). And, don't forget, this was way before steroids.

Dale Murphy should be in the Hall of Fame. That's my position. But, obviously, not everybody agrees with me. While acknowledging the facts I just presented, some will say his weaknesses are too great to merit Hall admittance. They will point out, for example, his high career strikeouts—1,748—his not-so impressive lifetime batting average of .265, and his decline in productivity at a relatively early age.

In response, I say he has more than made up for these weaknesses by his positive influence on the game and sports in general since his retirement, like founding iWontCheat.com, a nonprofit organization that encourages kids, parents, and coaches not to cheat by using performance enhancing drugs. I think he should be in the Hall of Fame, and I believe you should too.

Why am I telling you this? This isn't a book about baseball players who should have been elected to the Hall of Fame, after all. Why, then, take the time to debate the issue here? Because this is apologetics (what I call *giving answers*). What I just did on behalf of my hero, Dale Murphy, is, in effect, apologetics, the subject of this entire section.

Apologetics is a big word, but don't let it intimidate you. It comes from the Greek word *apologia*, which means "to defend." Any time you take a position on something—from politics, to movies, to Dale Murphy—someone will disagree with you. They will challenge your position, and you will have to defend it. I have a position about Dale Murphy (and I just happen to be right), but others disagree, so I must defend what I believe. When I do this, I'm engaging in apologetics.

I also take a position on Jesus Christ, the Christian Bible, and the Christian faith. I believe—as do you and millions of others on planet earth—that Jesus is the unique Son of God; that the Bible is God's singular, complete, and credible communication to man; and that Christianity is the world's only true, God-given faith system. Not everybody agrees with me, so I must defend what I believe.

Furthermore, as someone called to convert others, I must also use apologetics to help others overcome their objections to Christianity and put their faith in the Jesus of the Scriptures.

The Roles of Giving Answers (Apologetics)

Giving answers accomplishes two important objectives. First, it strengthens the faith of the believer. All of us have questions about our faith, nagging issues that exist in the back of our minds that make us wonder. Each of these is like a time bomb in our faith foundation. If we aren't careful, these time bombs can explode and destroy our faith. Over time, the doubts mount up, but the answers never come. So eventually we give up and walk away from Jesus altogether. Sadly, you and I both know people who were raised as Christians only to turn away from the faith because of questions

A Believer's Faith Foundation

that were never answered.

We can't afford to ignore the questions our friends at school, fellow Christians, children, or new disciples have about Christianity. Far from this, we must proactively identify and remove these doubts, solidifying their faith in God, the Bible, and Jesus. This is what giving answers can do.

The second critical use of giving answers is as an aid to conversion. Today, when someone glances at the cross, they see a stone wall. That wall represents the doubts they have about our faith. If we want them to take the cross seriously, we must tear down that wall and rebuild it on the other side, showing the lost that the truth always leads to the cross. Giving answers is our way of doing this.

Questions Destroy Our Foundation

One final note before we move on. It's important to understand that giving answers is not the gospel. In other words, it is not in itself God's good news of the way of salvation. Giving answers is only a tool to get people to take the good news seriously, to receive it as more than mythology or fairy tales. I've heard people say, "Nobody ever got saved through apologetics." While this may be true, I know many who have been lost without it.

Questions Create Stone Wall

Giving Answers in the Bible

The concept of giving answers is a biblical one. God, the Creator of our minds, has made us thinking, reasoning creatures. And while there is always a requirement for faith, it is not a blind faith. We believe in things we cannot see, but not in things of which we have no proof. Let me illustrate it

Giving Answers Moves Wall

for you.

You remember the movie *The Wizard of Oz*, I'm sure. Dorothy follows the Yellow Brick Road to see the Wizard. She takes the road in the first place because Glenda, the Good Witch of the North, and the Munchkins tell her to. As she walks, she sees signs that say, "Emerald City—This way," and she follows. The people who live along the road confirm the signs—Emerald City up ahead. Then, as she gets closer, she sees the city in the distance with the road heading in that direction. But she still can't actually *see the road entering the city*; her view is blocked by the rolling hills.

All of sudden, the Scarecrow stops her and says, "What if the road doesn't lead us to the city after all, Dorothy? We can't actually see it going into the city, you know." Dorothy replies, "Yes, you're right, Scarecrow. But we have plenty of evidence to support believing it does. Remember the Witch of the North told me it would take us there, and the signs along the way said it would, and even the people who lived along the road said it would. And now you can see for yourself that it heads off in that direction. No, we *can't see it actually entering the gates*, but we *have faith it will* because the evidence confirms that conclusion." Convinced, they continue, reach Emerald City, and meet the Wizard of Oz.

That's how the Christian faith works. We finish our journey with faith, but the evidence overwhelmingly confirms our conclusion.

So, does anyone in the Bible give answers? The short answer is yes. First, there are the explicit instructions. Many would point to 1 Peter 3:15, which reads, "But in your hearts set apart Christ as Lord. *Always be prepared to give an answer* to everyone who asks you to give the reason for the hope that you have." I'm not sure this is a command to do what we would traditionally call apologetics, or giving answers. It uses the Greek word, *apologia*, but Peter uses it when referring to claiming Christ in the context of persecution. Furthermore, if we only defended the faith when someone asked us, as the text clearly states, we wouldn't be giving a lot of answers. The fact is, most people just don't ask.

Perhaps a better direct text is 2 Corinthians 10:5 where Paul writes, "We demolish arguments and every pretension that sets itself up against the knowledge of God, and we take captive every thought to make it obedient to Christ." While the word apologia does not occur in this verse, the word arguments does.

This word literally means "reasonings," and the word demolish means "to wage war against."[5] So we are waging war against reasonings that set themselves up, or exalt themselves, against the knowledge of God. While Paul is probably talking about any argument that leads to unrighteousness or sin, the principle is very much applicable to giving answers in the traditional sense.

While the actual direct commandments to give answers may not be numerous, the examples of it taking place in Scripture are plentiful. Let me give you just three, starting with two lesser known examples and concluding with a famous one.

There's an intriguing example in the book of Joshua (4:1–9). Just after the people crossed the Jordan in a breathtaking miracle, God sent twelve men back into the riverbed. They were to find twelve stones and bring them back to the camp where Joshua would stack them. The Scripture tells us the reason God did this—to serve as a sign. These stones are to "serve as a sign among you. [So that] in the future, when your children ask you, 'What do these stones mean?' tell them that the flow of the Jordan was cut off before the ark of the covenant of the Lord" (6–7).

Now, why didn't God just have the eyewitnesses tell their children about this miraculous event years later? Certainly, people are expected to believe without *any proof*, right? Wrong. God knew these stones would serve as *evidence* that what the children were told was true, and if they didn't believe it, they could go back and check it out themselves. The writer even says, "And they are there *to this day*" (verse 9).

A second example comes from the words of Jesus in John 10:38. Jesus was having another confrontation with the Pharisees; they were objecting to his claims to deity (John 10:30). In his response to their unbelief, he says this, "Even though you don't believe me, *believe the miracles...*" Did you read that? *Believe the miracles.* In other words, he knew what he was claiming—that he was God in person—challenged their minds to the maximum. So he gave them *proof*, evidence, that his word was true, the miracles. If Jesus gives answers, shouldn't we?

Then, of course, there's St. Paul's famous passage in 1 Corinthians:

> For what I received I passed on to you as of first importance: that Christ died for our sins according to the Scriptures, that he was buried, that he was raised on the third day according to the Scriptures, and that he appeared to Peter, and then to the Twelve. After that, he appeared to more than five hundred of the brothers at the same time, *most of whom are still living*, though some have fallen asleep. Then he appeared to James, then to all the apostles, and last of all he appeared to

> me also, as to one abnormally born. (1 Corinthians 15:3–8)

So, again, why did Paul even say this? Apparently, some people were claiming that Jesus was not resurrected at all (15:12). Paul was defending this truth not by simply declaring it to be so louder than others were claiming it wasn't. *He offered proof.* He listed those who had actually seen him alive. Then, he went even further, claiming that many of them were *still* alive. Why? So if you were one who doubted, you could go check it out for yourself. Just like Joshua's twelve stones, Paul pointed skeptics to the evidence, in this case, the hundreds of eyewitnesses.

Starting Assumptions

Giving answers, overall, is about facts, evidence, and arguments—sharing information that isn't commonly reported about our faith or about false belief systems. But there is one thing we must keep in mind when considering facts and evidence: they don't speak for themselves.[6]

Everyone comes to the facts with a set of starting assumptions that color their view of facts. Some call this their "worldview" or "bias." Whether it's the facts about the preservation of the New Testament copies, the dinosaurs, dating methods, or God himself, we are all biased in some way.

Peter Galling of Answers in Genesis discusses this idea in relation to the creation/evolution issue, but it applies across the board. He writes the following:

> Much of the problem stems from the different *starting points* of creationists and Darwinists. Everyone, scientist or not, must start their quests for knowledge with some unprovable axiom—some *a priori* belief on which they sort

> through experience and deduce other truths. This starting point, whatever it is, can only be accepted by faith; eventually, in each belief system, there must be some unprovable, presupposed foundation for reasoning (since an infinite regression is impossible).
>
> For Bible-believing Christians, God's Word is our starting point: our presupposed foundation through which we interpret and balance fallen man's ideas, including those derived scientifically. Although some may consider this a foolish faith, *everyone* has such faith in *something*. But which is foolish: faith in the unmovable Word of the omniscient creator God or faith in man's fallible, changing ideas?[7]

The truth about starting assumptions will impact how those outside the faith accept the answers you give them. People in our culture are raised skeptical of Christianity and biased against its major teachings. Consequently, as you share answers with people, you may notice that many resist your ideas and always come up with another objection. Talking to them becomes a little like a verbal tennis match; no matter what you say, they have a comeback. If this happens, you may need to regroup and address the issue of starting assumptions before you can make any real headway with your answers. In fact, in some cases you may even want to begin here as well.

Also, keep in mind that bias toward Christianity is not always based on what one has been taught through the years. Sometimes questions or intellectual objections are only a smoke screen for the real issues. Some cling to objections because they have sin to hide; they have some lifestyle that they know is wrong but don't want to change. Perhaps they're living with their girlfriend, love porn, or are entangled in some immorality they don't want to give up. They don't want God telling them what to do, so they find a way to write off Scripture based on what they saw on television or read in high school biology. These are the sons and daughters of Psalm 2.

Then there's the person who rejects Christianity intellectually but is actually just defending themselves from pain in their past. The faith is off the table because some Christian years ago hurt them. They don't want to say this directly, so instead they use a false intellectual concern to justify their heart-born rejection.

Whatever the case, our job is the same: deal with the objection as if it were real. Once you deal with the intellectual issue, you'll be free to explore other possible causes. But if you don't deal with the question, you'll never know.

When you feel it's necessary, here's a simple way to take on the starting assumptions issue:

1. *Pray that God will open their eyes*, allowing them to consider evidence with a different set of starting assumptions (namely that the Bible is true) and recognize the bias they already have.

2. *Challenge them with the truth about starting assumptions and bias* when you discuss spiritual truth with them. Politely call them out on their bias and explain the role of starting assumptions to them. Ask them to consider the possibility that your answers are right in order to objectively consider them.

3. *Give them information to challenge their starting assumptions.* Make sure your answers are sound, reasonable, and well thought out. Be ready for counter arguments and always be kind and respectful in your discussions. Eventually, with the Spirit's help, you'll win the battle.

Conclusion

Apologetics means to give answers to the questions people are asking about Christianity. It is used not only to solidify the faith of the believer, but also to remove barriers that keep non-Christians from believing the gospel. This activity is used throughout Scripture and is a critical tool for extending the kingdom of God in our contemporary culture.

Now let's take a look at some important principles related to apologetics, what I call the "Seven Laws of Apologetics."

Chapter 7

The Seven Laws of Apologetics

Before you get started learning answers to common faith questions, I want to share with you some basic principles of apologetics, what I call the "Seven Laws of Apologetics." These are things I've picked up over the years that are important foundational principles you need to know before you enter the intellectual battlefield.

1. The other guy doesn't know as much as you think. Most people don't know what they're talking about. What they know is what they've been told all their lives, what they heard in biology class, or what they saw on some anti-Christian television show. They know the talking points of the world, but that's about it. When you get one layer deeper into a subject, you find their knowledge quickly comes to an end.

The point is you don't have to have a PhD in apologetics, or science, or history in order to overcome the objections of the average non-Christian. If you learn the material two or three layers deep, you'll know more than enough to do your job. So don't be intimidated. You can do this! You've been learning all your life and you're smart enough to learn this material as well.

2. Everybody has faith. Some non-Christians, especially those who are science-minded, think you operate by faith but they don't. They're more "reasonable," "intellectual," and base what they believe purely on what they can see, test, and verify. They're just about the facts...and you're not.

But don't be fooled by this "smarter-than-thou" attitude. Everybody has faith, even the scientist. As I'll explain later, science itself is based on assumptions that are faith-based in nature and cannot be proven by the scientific method. The reliability of the senses, the laws of logic, the existence of an objective reality outside of ourselves—all of these assumptions (among others) cannot be proven, but must be accepted by faith.

3. A contradiction can never be true. Many of the laws of logic are invaluable as you engage a world where thinking isn't what it used to be. But none is more important than the law of contradiction. Even if this is a new term to you, you use this principle every day. This law states that something cannot be both A and non-A at the same time and in the same relationship. It cannot be true that I am Wes Moore the author of this book and I am not Wes Moore the author of this book.

The reason this is so important to remember and recognize is that many people today accept this notion when it comes to spiritual things. As an example, non-Christians today (and, sadly, many Christians) think that all religions lead to the same God. But this is the classic case of saying a contradiction can be true. When you study the major teachings of the world's religions (on the nature of God, heaven and hell, salvation, man, Jesus, the Bible, etc.), you find they wildly and constantly contradict each other. Therefore, they can't all be true; they can't all lead to the same God.

4. Never say, "I don't know," twice. One of the sad truths about Christians today, especially in America, is that they're lazy. We'll put out our last ounce of energy for soccer, or college, or our lawn, but when it comes to the things of God and his work, we want somebody else to do the work for us. You can't do this and be successful at engaging the lost. You're going to have to work.

No matter how experienced you are, or how knowledgeable, you'll always get questions from an unbeliever that will stump you. People have so many issues and so many crazy ways of thinking, you can't possibly be ready for everything. And that's okay.

Don't let this fact discourage you. When you get a question you can't answer, don't give some half-thought-through answer. Make sure you know what your friend is saying and then say, "I'm not sure about that. But I'll research it and get back to you." Then go research the answer and bring it back to your friend.

A question you can't answer is actually a gift because it gives you the chance to learn something new and add it to your toolbox. But, whatever you do, don't waste the chance to learn. Don't be lazy and not get the answer. Then you'll violate this rule: Never say, "I don't know," twice.

The Seven Laws of Apologetics
1. The other guy doesn't know as much as you think.
2. Everybody has faith.
3. A contradiction can never be true.
4. Never say, "I don't know" twice.
5. Verify everything.
6. You've got to have proof.
7. Never get angry.

5. Verify everything. Most people don't know what they're talking about (Have I said that before?), even Christians. When someone tells you something new, whether it is in support of the faith or an attack against it, don't accept it until you've had the chance to validate it.

Christians use some pretty bad arguments and pass around half-truths all the time. They seem to support the Bible so we don't think anything of them. And then we go use them with the lost and look like fools (if they're smart enough to check us out too). A bad argument is a bad argument whether it defends the Bible or not.

Further, non-Christians make claims that have no basis or are only partly true as well. Later I talk about Asclepius, the Greek god of healing. Some people claim his myth formed part of the basis for the Jesus story, but when I actually read it for myself, I saw how ridiculous the claim really was.

That leads me to an important final point on this law: Read the source for yourself. In other words, if the argument is over what Charles Darwin said, read Darwin's writings yourself. If it's over a certain passage in the Bible, go read it *yourself.* I can't tell you how many times this has completely changed the argument. So much of the time—and I hate to beat a dead horse here—the other guy doesn't know what he's talking about.

6. You've got to have proof. Over the years, I've talked to some folks who have some wacky (even to non-Christians) ideas about spiritual things. Some of the thinking in the New Age movement is especially strange. Trying to show them the light is like trying to grab smoke in your hand.

With these kinds of people, I found myself trying to show them why I was right and they were wrong (which is still a good strategy), until it dawned on me to turn the tables a bit and put them on the defensive. Now sometimes my strategy is to ask them to prove to me that their crazy theories are right.

If God's a woman, give me your proof. If reincarnation is true, show me some evidence. If I am God and you are God and the trees are God, tell me how I can be sure. The harsh truth is, there is no proof; there's only wild conjecture by those who write books, supposed authorities who found their ideas on unsubstantiated theories.

And that's the point. You can't just believe something because you believe it. You need a reason to believe, some proof that your belief is to be preferred over fairies and pixy dust.

Christianity and the teachings of the Bible are rock solid when it comes to evidence, proof, and sound reasoning. So, when you engage people, ask them why they believe what they believe. Where's their proof? When they can't give any, ask them why their belief is better than belief in Greek mythology (or any other belief system we all know to be ridiculous), and then share with them the evidence for Christianity.

7. Never get angry. Get ready for it—the lost will tick you off. They'll say things that are outrageous or completely unfounded, and you'll feel this blood rush coming up from your chest. You'll want to pounce and destroy your target. But you can't! You've got to maintain your cool. Here's why it's always a bad idea to get angry when discussing issues of faith:

- *Anger escalates into arguing and conflict.* You can't help your friend see the light if you let things get out of hand. He'll be in a fighting mood, not a listening one.
- *Anger keeps you from understanding what he's really saying.* When you get red (that's what we called it when I was growing up), your ears get stopped up. You jump to conclusions and stop hearing your friend.
- *Anger keeps you from responding properly.* You can't think straight when you get mad. You start blurting out emotional responses instead of logical, reasonable arguments.

The best way I've found to control anger in these situations is to remember that this isn't a personal issue. It's about understanding what they really believe and then trying to show them the light. You want to hear the strange, outlandish ideas of the lost around you so you can help them see their error and find the truth.

Moving Ahead

By now you have a basic strategy to engage the lost in your sphere of influence (the REAP strategy) and you understand not only what apologetics is and its importance, but also some basic principles when it comes to using your apologetics (the "Seven Laws"). Now let's try to answer some of the most common questions and objections to the Christian faith.

The Spiritual Top 50:
50 Common Spiritual Questions & Answers

Top 50 Questions Table of Contents		
Chapter	*Category*	*Page*
8	God	93
9	Bible	103
10	Jesus	113
11	Science	123
12	Truth	135
13	Church and Christianity	143

Chapter 8
God Questions

God Questions	
1. How can I know God exists?	94
2. How can I know who God is and what he is like?	95
3. Aren't we all part of God?	96
4. Is God a she?	97
5. Why does God let people suffer?	97
6. God wouldn't send anyone to hell.	98
7. Hasn't science disproved God?	99
8. You don't have to believe in God to believe in right and wrong.	100

1.How can I know God exists?

There a number of ways we can know that God exists. Let me explain a few of them briefly:

Nothing can make itself. Every effect must have a cause. Our universe—this massive, beautiful, amazing universe—must have a cause. It can't make itself. It's impossible. So ultimately something had to bring it into existence.

A design requires a designer. Our universe, from the greatest galaxy to the smallest cell, shows a powerful and complicated design. A design only comes from a thinking, rational, conscious being, a designer.

We have a conscience. Every human being has an inner sense of right and wrong. Though we don't always agree on the specifics, we all try to justify our actions as "good," even terrorists. Where did this come from? What is its cause? God, our Creator. The Resurrection of Jesus Christ. Documented, verifiable miracles are a certain proof of God's existence. If there is no God, how can the laws of nature be suspended? Not only is the Resurrection a confirmation of God's existence, but also of Jesus' claims—why would God resurrect a liar? The witness of the heart. The Bible says, "What may be known about God is plain to [all men] because God has made it plain to them" (Romans 1:19). Next to the Christian, the atheist thinks more about God than anyone else. Why? Because he's always fighting against his inner knowledge that his Maker is out there.

So, who made God? No one. He simply exists. It is logically necessary because we can't go back in time forever. At some point, someone simply has to exist; someone must have the power of life within themselves. Interestingly, when God is asked to give his name, he says, "I am" (Exodus 3:14), which means in Hebrew "the Existing One."

2. How can I know who God is and what he is like?

There are certain things we can learn about God just by peering out our kitchen window. We can know God is powerful because the creation is so immense; we can know God is super-intelligent because the world demonstrates such intricate and complicated design; and we can know God is moral because of our inner sense of right and wrong.

Interestingly enough, the Bible tells us we can deduce things about God based on his creation:

> For since the creation of the world God's invisible qualities—his eternal power and divine nature—have been clearly seen, being understood from what has been made, so that men are without excuse. (Romans 1:20)

However, there are important limits to what creation can tell us about our Maker, just as there are limits to what a car can tell us about the engineer who designed it. For us to know more personal things about God—what he likes and dislikes, what causes him pain, his gender, his knowledge of the past, his plans for the future—he must tell us directly. In other words, there are some things we simply cannot know about God unless he tells us himself.

So, has God told us any of these things? Yes. The Bible claims to be a record of what God has said about himself. "All Scripture is God-breathed" is its profound claim (2 Timothy 3:16).

I know what's going through your head right now: But the Bible was written by men. What about the other gospels? What about the errors and contradictions? All of these are good questions, and, thankfully, there are good answers coming. Just keep reading.

3. Aren't we all part of God?

I wonder if those of you who are asking this question really understand all this worldview teaches about reality. The idea that "all is God and God is all," as some put it, though it has many forms today, originated in ancient Hinduism, and is also known as *pantheism*.[8]

This view of life holds that God is not personal or even knowable. In pantheism, God is "transcendent reality of which the material universe and human beings are only a manifestation."[9] In other words, God is not a person, with a will or personality, and cannot be understood by human beings.

Further, the life you are living today is not your first life, nor will it be your last. You are living but one of countless existences where you have been trying to earn your way to a higher state in your next cycle of birth, called *samsara*. Eventually you hope to become one with the impersonal, unknowable God.

Finally, suffering is an illusion caused by your false belief that you are an individual separate from the Ultimate Reality that is God. Suffering can only be eliminated through an increasing knowledge of one's oneness with that mindless Reality.

Let me mention a few concerns you should have with this worldview:

- If God does not have a will, he cannot help you. There is no one to turn to when you're in trouble.
- Who will love you? We all seek someone to love us. But a mindless entity cannot love.
- The Resurrection of Jesus Christ shows that God is personal and knowable, that he acts in time to help people, and that people are not reincarnated, but resurrected.

4. Is God a she?

As stated in answer to God Question 2, there are some things we cannot know about God unless he tells us directly. In terms of gender, the Bible (which claims to be God telling us about himself) clearly states that God is masculine, a "he." This doesn't mean that being female is less "godly." After all, God created women and loves and values them just as he does men. And he gave them uniquely feminine qualities, qualities that flow from his perfect nature, though he is distinctly masculine.

This question touches on the whole concept of God's nature. In addition to those who teach that God is a "she," there are those who teach that God is in all of us and in nature. God, in their view, is "mother earth," or some kind of combined, mindless consciousness of man, animal, and the natural world. God is not a person, with a personality and a will, but a presence in us all.

What I ask of those who hold this view is to show me your proof that God has these kinds of attributes. You have to have a reason for your beliefs. You can't just believe something because you believe it. That's irrational and absurd—that's not only *blind* faith, it's *ignorant* faith (no offense intended). Why? Because you can never know you're right. You can't say your belief is any more valid than believing in fairies or pixie dust.

In fact, the evidence shows the opposite. The same reasoning we use every day tells us that God must have a mind and a will, and that he cannot be a part of creation (see God Question 1).

5. Why does God let people suffer?

To understand why death and suffering exist, you must understand two simple truths:

1. We have been separated from God, our source of life, allowing death to enter.

2. Our separation is not based on God's choice, but ours.

The first man, Adam, refused the Creator's command and brought death to all creation (Genesis 3:17-19). You might ask why God would allow us to suffer death in the first place. Why didn't he stop Adam or rescind his sentence? At some level, the answer is a mystery; I can't say for sure, and I'm not sure the Bible does either. However, there are a few things I can say for certain.

First, God allowed it to fulfill his ultimate purpose in creating. His ultimate purpose was not to provide us with a "cushy pillow life," but to demonstrate the full glory of his nature. Evil, death, and suffering demonstrate, among other things, the excellencies of his justice, mercy, patience, and grace.

Second, God allowed it to bring about a good otherwise not possible. The Bible is replete with illustrations of this. An excellent example of this is the death of Jesus Christ.

Finally, God has done more about it than anyone. He limits evil and suffering now, he commands his people to labor to meet the needs of those who are hurting, and he died so it could be fully and finally eliminated (Jesus Christ on the cross). Perhaps best of all, one day he promises no more (Revelation 21:4)!

6. God wouldn't send anyone to hell.

Here are a few things to think about when considering this question.

In the first place, why wouldn't God send anyone to hell?

Whether by execution or life in prison, we punish criminals severely when their crimes justify it. Why can't God? Second, don't place your own sense of morality above your Creator's. Be very careful when you think of elevating your changing, culturally influenced, and often corrupt moral compass over the unchanging, independent, pure moral nature of God.

Finally, to grasp the reasonableness of hell, you must understand the holiness of God. Holy means "separate or transcendent." God's nature—his sense of morality, justice, and judgment—is infinitely higher than ours. He's on another level altogether. We're like pee-wee league football, and he's the best team in the NFL.

To us, a moral slip isn't that big a deal. After all, we can honestly say we've been there before, or at least as sinners, we can understand. Only the most heinous of crimes move us. But God's moral sensitivity is not so numb. He has never sinned; he is completely pure; he is infinitely offended with each moral lapse.

One famous confession says this: "The Lord our God is... infinite in being and perfection...who only hath immortality, dwelling in the light which no man can approach unto; who is immutable, immense, eternal, incomprehensible, almighty, every way infinite, most holy, most wise, most free, most absolute."[10]

A proper understanding of hell is required for a proper understanding of God.

7. Hasn't science disproved God?

Science can't possibly disprove God. To say for certain there is no God, you'd have to be everywhere in the universe at the same time—you'd have to be God to say he didn't exist!

Furthermore, scientists must assume the biblical God exists (even if they don't believe in him) and operates as the Bible says in order to do science at all.[11] Uniformity of nature, laws of logic, and the reliability of our senses (to name a few) are all *assumed* when science is performed, but evolutionary theory does not explain why these exist in the first place. How can uniformity come out of chance and chaos? (Ever seen an explosion produce order?) How do immaterial laws of logic exist in a material-only universe? And how can we be sure our senses are reliable if we evolved by chance? (Maybe yours are and mine aren't?)

However, the biblical worldview explains why these three things exist. The universe is uniform because the Creator made it that way in the beginning and promises to sustain it (Genesis 1:1, Hebrews 1:3, Numbers 23:19, Psalm 139:7-8); laws of logic reflect the way God thinks (Genesis 1:26, Ephesians 5:1, 2 Timothy 2:13, Colossians 2:3); and our senses are reliable because the Creator made them for the very purpose of understanding the universe he had created (Genesis 1:28).

The universe cannot be separated from God. It relies on his nature to exist. He is the foundation, and the creation is the house. His mind and nature form the outline of our existence (logic, morality, uniformity); his power upholds our existence (moral, physical, and spiritual).

8. You don't have to believe in God to believe in right and wrong.

No, you don't. Everybody believes in right and wrong, even terrorists. In fact, this is one of the ways we can know God exists and is a moral being. The question isn't whether or not you *can* believe in right and wrong, but how do you *justify* your belief. For example, when you say, "Murder is wrong," how do you know? *Why* is murder wrong?

You could say because most people say it is, but there have been times when most people believed it was wrong to free slaves. You could say this is what you were taught growing up, but why does that matter? Maybe your parents were wrong. You could say because the law says so, but laws have been passed that legalized the killing millions of Jews, something we know to be wrong.

You could say that it inhibits our evolution. But are you sure? How does keeping a child with a mental disorder alive move us down the path of evolutionary excellence? And what about survival of the fittest? Take a long, hard look into those words before you say anything is wrong. If it promotes my survival, why shouldn't it be right? I survive. You die. Evolution at work.

There must be a final, absolute standard for us to make claims about right and wrong. And the only absolute standard is God. God, our Creator, exercising his absolute right, declares it to be so. In the case of murder, God made us in his image and therefore murder is wrong.

Chapter 9
Bible Questions

Bible Questions	
1. The Bible is full of contradictions and errors.	104
2. The Bible was written by man--how can anyone trust it?	104
3. God commanded genocide in the Old Testament.	105
4. The Bible promotes slavery.	106
5. The Old Testament and New Testament describe different Gods.	107
6. What about the other gospels?	108
7. The Ten Commandments were copied from other cultures.	109
8. Isn't the Bible open to interpretations?	110
9. The Bible is homophobic.	111

1. The Bible is full of contradictions and errors.

First, I'd like to ask you to name an error or contradiction in the Bible. Please be specific. Okay, now name another. Can you think of a third?

Undoubtedly, some of you can name specifics, but many people who make this charge cannot. They are simply repeating what they have heard in the culture all their lives, but have never really investigated and confirmed for themselves. They simply assume the Bible is wrong from the outset. And that's my point.

As you work through the answers in this book, challenge yourself to acknowledge the biases you have, even if you haven't recognized them as such before. Labor to give the arguments made in this book a fair hearing and not just assume they're wrong because you've already concluded the Bible isn't true.

Regarding specific alleged contradictions and errors, let me briefly address two so you can see that there are solid answers to common complaints.

The existence of Nazareth, Jesus' hometown. Some have charged that Nazareth never existed in the time of Jesus. However, a list of priests relocating after the fall of Jerusalem in A. D. 70 was found. One of them is listed as having settled in Nazareth.[12]

The existence of the Hittite people from the Old Testament. Critics have disputed the existence of this ancient people group. But the discovery of the Hittite library in Turkey in 1906 dismantled this claim.[13]

2. The Bible was written by man—how can anyone trust it?

This question assumes that God cannot produce something reliable if humans are involved. This is irrational. When you come to see that God must be, and that he must have a super-intelligent mind, a free and creative will, and immense power—just as the Bible says—then concluding he cannot manage human beings in the writing and preservation of a single book becomes absurd.

How exactly was the Bible written? First, God used men to write down the words, but not as puppets on a string. He used their personalities, passions, experiences, and ideas in creating his "Word." However, he oversaw the process in such a way that what was produced in the end was exactly what he wanted. This process is called *inspiration*.

Furthermore, the evidence doesn't support the charge that the Bible is untrustworthy. The Bible is the most well-documented book of all antiquity. The New Testament alone has more supporting manuscripts in the original language than any other book in the world (more than 5,000).[14] The closest competitor is Homer's *Iliad* with 643.[15]

Not only this, but the Bible is the most well-preserved book we have today. The Dead Sea Scrolls are a large collection of ancient writings found in caves near the Dead Sea. More than 200 biblical manuscripts were found there, all approximately 1,000 years older than any previously discovered.[16] The comparison of these copies with ones dated much later reveals that in spite of repeated copying through the centuries, the biblical texts remained almost identical.

Bottom line: you can trust the Bible.

3. God commanded genocide in the Old Testament.

Many refuse to believe in the God of the Bible because they do not approve of God's command to kill the nations of Canaan (the Canaanites, also referred to generally as the Amorites) during the Old Testament period. In their minds, either God is an evil tyrant, or the Jews simply made him up to justify their warmongering. Let me give you a few things to think about here.

First, God's destruction of the Canaanites was not arbitrary, but was a direct result of their extreme wickedness, which included child sacrifice (Deuteronomy 12:29-31, Psalm 106:34-38).

Second, God did not carry out his judgment until their evil had reached its full measure; he even made the Jews wait 400 years to take the land so his punishment would be justified (Genesis 15:16).

Third, the sin of the Canaanites was further multiplied because they had the knowledge of the true God in their history. Canaan, the father of the Canaanites, was Noah's grandson (Genesis 9:18, 10:15-18). As Americans, we should take this example to heart.

Fourth, God has the authority to take life. It is not unrighteous for the giver of life to take it when he sees fit. At the end of time, he will take many lives for the same reason he took the Canaanite's—immorality.

Finally, regarding the slaughter of innocent children, remember, "Death is not the ultimate destiny of the human race, nor is it the greatest evil. Someday God will give a full explanation, which is something only He can do."[17]

4. The Bible promotes slavery.

Why doesn't the Bible outlaw slavery altogether? Here are a few things to consider:

1. *Our impression of slavery—from American history—is not*

the same as the ancient practice. When we think of slavery, we think of people who were kidnapped and sold into lifelong cruelty. On the whole this was outlawed by ancient governments, and expressly forbidden by the Bible (Exodus 21:12-27).[18]

2. *Slavery in the Roman Empire was frequently a road to freedom and a better life.* "Life in slavery, at least with a decent master, could be more predictable and less demanding than the life of a poor free person. Since Romans often freed their salves, and since freed slaves of Roman citizens typically received Roman citizenship, one could improve his social status through enslavement."[19]

3. *God limited the abuses of slavery.* The Bible protected slaves from prostitution, abuse, and murder (Exodus 21:7-12, 26-27). Kidnapping a free person for slavery was punishable by death (Exodus 21:16), and denounced by Paul as evil (1 Timothy 1:10).

4. *God took a wise, long-term approach to slavery's eradication.* God laid the foundation for slavery's demise by teaching that owners and slaves are brothers (Philemon), and both the slave and free man are the same to him (Galatians 3:28). Given the economic situation of the first century, immediate and full eradication might have brought about greater suffering than the institution of slavery itself.

5. The Old Testament and New Testament describe different gods.

There's a popular notion that as humanity's view of God evolved, so the description of the biblical God evolved with it. In days past, humans saw God as vengeful, harsh, and cruel—so the God of the Old Testament was written that way—but as time went by they began to conceive of God as more loving, patient, and merciful— hence the loving God of the New Testament.

However, when you look at the data, there is clearly only one God whose nature and actions are consistent in both testaments.

The severe God of the New Testament. While certainly loving, the God of the New Testament executed Ananias and Sapphira for lying to him (Acts 5:1-11); put to death a political leader, Herod, for refusing to give him glory (Acts 12:19-23); and promised a "bed of suffering" for those who caused his people to sin and "intense suffering" for those of his people who practiced evil (Revelation 2:22-23).

The loving God of the Old Testament. While certainly severe, the God of the Old Testament spared an entire city out of concern for its children and animals (Jonah 4:10-11); instructed his followers to leave part of their harvest for the "alien, the fatherless, and the widow" (Deuteronomy 24:19); and destroyed his own people for refusing to seek justice, encourage the oppressed, and defend the fatherless and widows (Isaiah 1:17).

6. What about the other gospels?

We live in a conspiracy theory culture where even the Bible does not escape the eye of the cynic. They charge that a host of legitimate descriptions of Jesus' life—other gospels—were kept out of the New Testament (NT) by power-hungry church leaders.

First, the books to be included in the NT were determined by the early churches, not by any official Council (such as the Council of Nicaea). The list of twenty-seven books in our modern NT was already accepted by the people of God by the end of the first century, long before any church councils ever met.[20]

Second, books were kept out not for political reasons but because of who wrote them and what they taught.[21] The first requirement was that each book be written by an apostle or close associate. Books written under a pseudonym or too late to meet this requirement were rejected. Furthermore, many books were disqualified because of their teachings. A host of the rejected gospels were written by a group called the Gnostics. Here's what they believed:

> [Gnostics] regard this world as the creation of a series of evil archons or powers who wish to keep the human soul trapped in an evil physical body...preaches a hidden wisdom...only to a select group as necessary for salvation and escape from this world.[22]

From what you know about the NT, I'm sure you can see why they would have excluded teachings like this.

There is no conspiracy. The early Christians acted wisely and with integrity when filtering God's writings from fakes and frauds.

7. The Ten Commandments were copied from other cultures.

Some charge that the Ten Commandments (TC) are not original to the Jews but were copied from either the Egyptian Book of the Dead (BOD), an ancient guide for the afterlife, or Hammurabi's Code, an ancient law code.

When you hear this type of claim, remember that the differences are often far greater than the likenesses. Critics take loose similarities and act as if they are word-for-word replicas.

Furthermore, God has given us all the same moral code

written on our hearts, the conscience. Therefore, it would not be surprising to see moral directives reflect some of the same tenets at different times and in different cultures.

Chapter 125 of the BOD tells the dead person to make forty-two moral declarations when they encounter the gods in the after-life.[23] Some of the statements are similar to the Bible, like, "I have not killed." But there is much more different about them than the same. Consider the following comparisons and questions:

- The BOD is a confession to make after one dies; the TC are instructions for living.
- The BOD has forty-two directives; the TC have only ten.
- The BOD does not contain any mention of the first four commandments.
- The basic language and words used by the BOD and TC are not the same.
- Why didn't the Jews just copy the entire document as-is, since they lived in Egypt for the previous 400 years?
- Why did the Jews choose only one God when the BOD mentions forty-two?
- Why didn't the Jews use all negative statements like the BOD?

8. Isn't the Bible open to interpretation?

How do you understand the newspaper? How do you know the reporter is talking about a real flood in Iowa? Maybe he means it metaphorically. It's not a real flood; it's a flood of emotion, or a flood of corn, or a flood of political activism. Maybe he doesn't mean that at all. Who knows? You decide what you want him to mean and I'll decide what I want him to mean.

Yes, that makes absolutely no sense. Why? Because we know the reporter had an intent when he wrote, a meaning, and we know we can understand that meaning if we pay attention to the context (the words used before and after, the historical setting, the type of literature used, the recipient of the message, and other clues).

The Bible is no different. The Bible was written by authors who had a message to communicate, a message they wanted us to understand. And we can understand that message by paying attention to the context.

It may sound complicated, but we do it every day. We know when someone is kidding or serious; we know when they are telling us the history of Rome or giving us directions to the grocery store.

So what happens when we stop trying to understand the author's meaning, and we let the reader or hearer decide for themselves? The instant we do this we make communication impossible because then any statement can mean *anything at all*, and when this happens it really means nothing at all.

9. The Bible is homophobic.

I assume by this you mean the Bible promotes violence and hatred toward homosexuals.

First of all, it is not hatred to declare an action to be morally wrong. If I say prostitution is wrong, does that mean I hate prostitutes? No, of course not.

Second, you need to study the true intentions of this movement. We are told it is simply to give homosexuals "rights." But this isn't the full story. Search for "1972 Gay Rights Platform" on the Internet and read the stated goals of this movement. Pay special attention to numbers 3, 6, 7, and 8 from the state law section.

Third, the Bible does not condone violence toward or hatred for homosexuals. Jesus showed compassion to all types of sinners, including prostitutes and adulterers. Furthermore, he died to save people caught in sexual oppression. While I have never struggled with homosexual feelings, I have had sex before marriage and wrestled with pornography on and off for years. Yet God loves me and continues to help me overcome my struggles.

Finally, you need to understand that the Bible is clear that this desire and act are sinful. Critics often poke fun at Leviticus which says that homosexuality and eating shellfish are "detestable" before God (11:9-12). But what many don't know is that shellfish have more parasites than fish with fins, so they're a greater health risk. God promised to protect the Israelites from disease. This is how he did it.

Just like disease, moral sickness can also destroy a nation. Homosexuality, bestiality, adultery, and prostitution are forbidden, not out of hatred, but in order to protect the health of the community.

Chapter 10
Jesus Questions

Jesus Questions	
1. How do we even know Jesus existed?	114
2. Jesus never claimed to be divine.	115
3. Jesus was a good teacher, but not God.	115
4. What about all those who don't hear about Jesus?	116
5. Jesus was never resurrected.	117
6. The story of Jesus was influenced by earlier myths and religious accounts.	118
7. Christ is your "indwelling divinity" or your "God essence."	119
8. Wasn't Jesus' primary teaching to love each other in spite of our differences?	120
9. Jesus and Christ are not the same.	121

1. How do we know Jesus even existed?

Let's not discount the New Testament itself as eyewitness proof of Jesus' existence. It records the words of many different authors, written at different times in different places. Their testimony is found in the most well-preserved collection of documents of all antiquity, the New Testament.

Outside the New Testament, here are several non-Christian accounts of the existence of a man named Jesus in the first century[24]:

- Cornelius Tacitus (A.D. 55-120), a famous Roman historian, wrote in *Annals*, "Christus [a common misspelling of Christ], the founder of the name, was put to death by Pontius Pilate, procurator of Judea in the reign of Tiberius..."
- Lucian of Samosata, a Greek artist of the late second century, wrote, "The Christians, you know, worship a man to this day—the distinguished personage who introduced their novel rites, and was crucified on that account..."
- Suetonius, a Roman historian, wrote in *Life of Claudius*, "As the Jews were making constant disturbances at the instigation of Chrestus [another spelling of Christ], he [Claudius] expelled them from Rome."
- Pliny the Younger, governor of Bithynia in Asia Minor, wrote to Emperor Trajan in A.D. 112 concerning the number of Christians he was putting to death. At one point he said he "made them curse Christ, which a genuine Christian cannot be induced to do."

Note that these sources mention Jesus' death under Pontius Pilate, his crucifixion, and the loyalty of his followers, all key New Testament teachings.

2. Jesus never claimed to be divine.

Where's the proof that Jesus himself claimed to be God? There are several direct and indirect ways to show that Jesus did indeed believe he was God in human form.

1. *He accepted worship (Matthew 28:9).* A good Jew knew that only God could rightly accept worship. Yet many times Jesus was worshipped by his followers, but he never turned them away.

2. *He forgave sins (Mark 2:5-12).*[25] In this passage in Mark, Jesus forgave the sins of a sick man. The Jewish religious leaders quickly recognized the implication. "Why does this fellow talk like that?" they pondered. "Who can forgive sins but God alone?" But Jesus didn't back down.

3. *He claimed the title Son of Man (Mark 2:10, Daniel 7:13-14).*[26] Many people think the reference "Son of Man" has to do with Jesus' humanity, but it doesn't. By taking this name for himself, Jesus was reaching back into the Old Testament to the book of Daniel and grabbing a title of God from one of Daniel's great visions.

4. *He claimed the title I am (John 8:58, Exodus 3:14).* Finally, Jesus claimed another title reserved only for God. In fact, when Jesus told the Jewish leaders that he was I am, he was taking the first name God gave himself when he appeared to the Jewish people. When Moses asked God what his name was, he said, "I am who I am. This is what you are to say to the Israelites, 'I am has sent me to you'" (Exodus 3:14).

3. Jesus was a good teacher, but not God.

Think about what you're saying. In the last question, I

showed you how Jesus himself clearly claimed to be God. In the last 2,000 years, millions of people have given up everything—some life itself—to follow him. But if he wasn't what he claimed, then he was a liar and a deceiver. How can he then be a good teacher?

Most people say this as a form of religious political correctness. They know many people hold Jesus in high esteem so they don't want to completely dismiss him. Instead, they cleverly accept and reject him at the same time with this spiritual double talk.

Let me ask you a question: Why is it so unacceptable to you that Jesus is actually God? It might be that if he is, the religion you've followed all your life is wrong, and you can't accept that. Or maybe your parents or friends will turn away from you if you follow this Jesus guy.

But for many of you, these issues are only secondary. The real reason is if Jesus is God, then his words have authority over your life. God is real and he has a moral standard, and you hate that thought. You like running your own life and deciding for yourself what is right and wrong.

But is your life really going so well? Is following your "heart" really satisfying you? Are porn and greed and conflict such great paths? You might just find that following Jesus Christ is the most liberating thing you've ever done.

4. What about all those who don't hear about Jesus?

This is a fairness question. If Jesus is the only way to God, what about all those who haven't heard about him? Will they just be condemned to hell never having had a chance?

First, nobody is innocent. Whether we hear about Jesus or not, we have all violated God's moral standard and are guilty.

Second, the gospel has been preached all over the world for 2,000 years. Ninety-eight percent of the world's population has access to the Bible in their own language.[27]

Third, if someone wants to find the true God, then God will get the message to them. For an example of this, see the story of Cornelius in Acts 10.

Fourth, Christians believe that children who die are taken into God's grace automatically, forgiven of their sins, and given eternal life. The Bible gives us a beautiful picture of this in the Old Testament. After the death of King David's newborn son, he said these words, "*I will go to him*, but he will not return to me" (2 Samuel 12:23).

Finally, if you live in America (and especially if you are reading this book), you don't have this excuse. You have heard, many times perhaps, and now the ball is in your court. Here are the steps to take to be right with God: 1) repent of your sins, 2) trust that only Christ's death can save you, and 3) commit to serve Christ with the rest of your life.

5. Jesus was never resurrected.

If Jesus wasn't resurrected, he can't be God or the Savior of mankind, and Christianity becomes a crumbling house of cards. However, if he was...well, you know what that means.

As you can imagine, every aspect of the resurrection account has been criticized, yet millions still believe. Why? Because the objections don't overcome the powerful evidence and reasoning that supports his resurrection.

Here are brief answers to the top three claims:

1. *Jesus never died.* He was scourged, a cruel, bloody beating which made him too weak to carry his own cross (Mark 15:21). Just after he died, soldiers pierced his side with a spear, releasing blood and water, a clear sign of death (John 19:34). Pilate even sent soldiers to confirm he was dead (Mark 15:44).

2. *The disciples stole the body.* If so, the body was never found, though his enemies certainly would have searched for it. All they would have had to do to kill Christianity forever was to produce the body. Yet they never could. Furthermore, Pilate set a guard to make sure the body couldn't be stolen (Matthew 27:62-66).

3. *The disciples made it up.* After this deception, they knowingly taught and died for a lie. You may die for a lie you believe to be true, but you would never die for a lie you know to be a lie. "And they were willing to spend the rest of their lives proclaiming this, without any payoff from a human point of view.... They faced a life of hardship. They often went without food, slept exposed to the elements, were ridiculed, beaten, imprisoned. And finally, most of them were executed in tortuous ways."[28]

6. The story of Jesus was influenced by earlier myths and religious accounts.

People around the world claim that the story of Jesus was manufactured by borrowing from world religions and myths that predated him. From Buddhism, to Zoroastrianism, to Greek mythology, Christianity came about by combining elements of various other faith accounts to create the Jesus fable.

In all cases, you'll find these common flaws in their logic:

- The assumption that the New Testament is wrong. The critics' bias precludes any possibility other than this.

- The assumption that the New Testament authors were liars, in spite of their clear teaching to the contrary. Why build a religion of truth-telling on a foundation of lies and deceit?
- The assumption of the evolution of the "god concept." We start by assuming we are evolving, building on what was developed in the past, and forming a better god along the way.
- The assumption that similarity equals progeny. The critic assumes that if there are any similarities, Christianity must find its partial or full origin in the similar religion or myth. However, in the process, glaring dissimilarities are overlooked.

As an illustration of this last point, consider Asclepius, the Greek god of healing and medicine. One website claims Jesus was virtually identical to Asclepius, but ignores the marked differences.[29] His mother, Coronis, was a mortal who slept with Apollo. When she was unfaithful, she was murdered by Artemis, Apollo's sister, and placed on a funeral pyre. At the last minute, Apollo saved his unborn son and gave him to a centaur named Chiron who became his tutor.[30]

This kind of absurd comparison is common with these types of claims.

7. Christ is your "indwelling divinity" or "God-essence."[31]

The view of Jesus has changed so much that he isn't even a real person anymore, only a state of mind, a "vehicle to pure consciousness."[32] Is this so? Did the Bible get it wrong?

If this is the real Jesus, I'd like to see the evidence. What proof is there that Jesus isn't who the gospels say he is? In the writings that offer this theory, not a single shred of evidence is given, except a list of statements of the historical Jesus taken out of context.

For example, one author says Christ is not eternal because

"there is no past or future in Christ."[33] As proof for this, he quotes Christ's statement in John 8:58, "Before Abraham was, I am," and then says, "He did not say: 'I already existed before Abraham was born.'"[34] Yet, when you read the actual account, this is exactly what Jesus was saying.

In verse 56, Jesus had just said that Abraham saw his (Jesus') entrance into the world. The Jews then asked how he could know what Abraham saw since he was too young to have even met Abraham. Jesus answered with the statement, "I am," taking the name God gave himself in Exodus 3:14. This name means, "The Existing One."

Moreover, the actual evidence militates against this view of Jesus. From the context of his words, to the eyewitnesses of his death and resurrection—the proof points away from the "Christ-essence" theory.

Furthermore, the absurdity of the teachings that accompany this view of Christ—pain, problems, and death as illusions, for example[35]—seriously damage the credibility of this teaching.

8. Wasn't Jesus' primary teaching to love each other in spite of our differences?

Some people say that Jesus' overarching teaching was love, and that we should take this teaching and leave out the divisive talk about doctrines and dogmatic beliefs about God, the Bible, or other religions.

Indeed, like no other teacher in history Jesus taught us to love. He even taught us to show love to our enemies, regardless of their beliefs or lifestyle (Matthew 5:43-48).

But that's not all Jesus taught. The same Jesus who said to love others also said that God desires to be worshipped in truth, not in error (John 4:23); this same Jesus said that false teachers would come into the world and claim to be saviors in an effort to deceive (Mark 13:22).

The Jesus who taught love also made harsh moral judgments on many occasions, like when he called the people a "wicked and adulterous generation" (Matthew 12:39). And the loving Jesus taught many times about the fearful reality of a final day of Judgment (Matthew 25:31-46) and the awful experience of being condemned to hell (Luke 16:19-31).

So my question for you is this: How do you decide which parts of Jesus' teaching to accept and which to reject? The same book that tells us of his love for all, also tells us of his strong moral stance, his unwavering commitment to the one God, and his deep conviction of hell for the wicked.

Could it be that you've chosen the kind of Jesus—and by extension, the kind of God—you've wanted all along? We don't mind a God who tells us to love others, but we can't stand the kind of God who tells us what is right and wrong, and promises one day to judge us by the standard he sets.

9. Jesus and Christ are not the same.

It is a common charge today that the words "Jesus Christ" do not represent a single person. Jesus, they say, was a real man of history; Christ, however, is not referring to the man Jesus, but the spiritual energy or God-presence indwelling us all. Eckhart Tolle puts it this way:

> [Jesus] had gone beyond the consciousness dimension governed by time, into the realm of the timeless... Thus, the man Jesus became Christ, a vehicle for pure consciousness.[36]

This view is popular in New Age spirituality, a belief system rooted in ancient Hinduism, where the ultimate goal is to attain oneness with an impersonal, divine force, the Ultimate Reality.

This view of Christ, like all New Age teachings, is based on two core beliefs: 1) man has entered a new age of evolution where his spiritual powers will be increased, and 2) the original teachings of Jesus were distorted by his disciples and are unreliably preserved in the writings of the New Testament (NT).[37]

In answer to this teaching, let me first explain the difference between "Jesus" and "Christ" as defined in the NT. Jesus means "Jehovah is salvation" and is the name given to the firstborn son of Mary and Joseph from Nazareth in Palestine. Christ means "anointed one" and represents the man Jesus' title, not a divine presence or energy.

In terms of weaknesses, first of all, human evolution is not happening. The Big Bang does not explain our origins, mutations and natural selection are going the wrong way, scientific dating methods are deeply flawed, and the fossil record is fraught with problems (see Science Questions 1-4).

Furthermore, the evidence doesn't support the charge that Jesus' teachings were distorted and are not reliably preserved in the NT.

Chapter 11
Science Questions

Science Questions	
1. The Big Bang proves the Bible isn't true.	124
2. What about mutations and natural selection?	125
3. Scientific dating methods have proven the Bible isn't true.	126
4. The fossil record proves the Bible is wrong.	127
5. What about the dinosaurs?	128
6. The Genesis creation account was taken from other cultures.	129
7. There is no evidence of a global flood.	130
8. Miracles are scientifically impossible.	131
9. Great scientists, like Galileo, have been persecuted by the church.	132

1. The Big Bang proves the Bible isn't true.

To properly evaluate the Big Bang, first you need to understand that there are two types of science. *Observational* science is based on observable, repeatable events in the present. *Origins* science is not based on observation, but takes present facts and develops theories to explain those facts. Origins science is heavily influenced by the scientist's worldview.

The Big Bang and creation are both origins science because they deal with the past.

The Big Bang has many weaknesses. Even secular (non-religious) scientists are beginning to question the validity of this theory. Visit www.cosmologystatement.org to read "An Open Letter to the Scientific Community" signed by 218 scientists and engineers.[38]

Here are some well known problems with the Big Bang model:

- "The known laws of physics fail to describe how the singularity could exist."[39]
- The law of cause and effect is violated. The Big Bang provides no answer for the cause of the explosion.[40]
- When matter is created, an equal amount of antimatter is created. But "the visible universe is comprised almost entirely of matter—with only trace amounts of antimatter anywhere."[41]
- Though galaxies in the distant universe should appear in the early stages of development (because we are seeing them billions of years ago), "images from the Hubble Deep Field show fully-formed galaxies in the early universe."[42]

The Bible provides a scientifically sound explanation of our origins given by an eyewitness: God.[43]

2. What about mutations and natural selection?

In evolutionary theory, life starts off in simple forms and evolves into more complex ones over time. Consequently, for evolution to be true, information must be added to our DNA over time.

Evolutionists propose two mechanisms to do this: mutations and natural selection. However, in observational science, mutations and natural selection only *reduce the amount of genetic information.*

Mutations. A mutation is a copying mistake in DNA which causes changes in life. Some mutations have no effect, some are unnoticeable, while others produce significant changes.

Mutations, although helpful sometimes, don't add information. Take the wingless beetle. On a windy island it may be beneficial for a beetle to have a mutation that causes the loss of wings. However, it's a *loss of information* for wings that made the beetle more likely to survive, not an addition.[44]

Natural Selection. Natural selection can be defined as "the process by which individuals possessing a set of traits that confer a survival advantage in a given environment tend to leave more offspring."[45]

If we go back to our wingless beetle, natural selection would prefer the wingless beetle because it would have an advantage over the beetles with wings. However, remember: 1) only beetles are produced through this process (not another type of life) and 2) no new information was added to the beetle's DNA.

The Biblical Model Fits Better. The biblical model fits what we observe in real science better. God, an infinite intelligence, created all of life with the genetic information required to develop into the life we see today.

Further, God created different *kinds* of animals who then reproduced after their kinds (dogs to dogs, cats to cats, etc.). From this original kind, through natural selection and other processes, the various forms of life we see today developed.

3. Scientific dating methods prove the Bible isn't true.

The Bible teaches only thousands of years (about 6,000). Secular science teaches billions (about 14 billion). They both can't be true. So, is the world really billions of years old or only thousands?

There are many physical processes that can be used to calculate the age of the world, most of which contradict secular science. If we measure the amount of salt in the sea and calculate the net increase in saltiness per year, we can work backward and determine the maximum possible age of the oceans (not the actual age), sixty-two million years, many times less than the billions reported in science textbooks.[46]

Radiometric dating (RD), a method of dating rocks from lava flows that supposedly lock down the billions of years dates, are based on unproven assumptions: 1) that all the starting conditions are known, 2) that the decay rate of the radioisotopes hasn't changed, and 3) that the system is closed, allowing no addition or deletion of material. And all of this *over millions or billions of years!*[47]

Furthermore, RD methods are not always accurate for rocks of known ages and different methods often disagree when dating the same sample.[48]

Ultimately, the best way to determine the age of the earth

is to ask an eyewitness: God. He was there when the world and life were created. So, the ultimate question is who are you going to trust—man or God?

4. The fossil record proves the Bible is wrong.

The fossil record is another central pillar in the argument for the evolution of life (an argument against the validity of the Bible). But it is not the only valid theory that explains the evidence. There is also Noah's flood.

You must understand that what we *actually see* in the fossil record is simply the *order of burial* of certain plants and animals. What we *conclude* from that order—that it represents the order of the evolution of life—is our *interpretation* of what we see. Contrary to popular notions, the fossil record as interpreted by evolutionists is fraught with problems. Here are a few:

- "The impeccable state of preservation of most fossils requires the animals and plants to have been very rapidly buried."[49] Plants or animals buried slowly over long periods would be destroyed by scavengers and bacteria.[50]
- Large fossil graveyards found all over the world cannot be explained by slow, gradual processes. "The Redwall Limestone of the Grand Canyon contains... marine creatures buried by fast-moving slurry that involved 24 cubic miles of lime, sand, and silt. No river or lake today can account for the scale of these graveyards."[51]
- Polystrate fossils (fossils that cut vertically through many geologic layers), like the trees at Joggins, Nova Scotia, are not easily explained by slow, gradual fossilization.[52]

The biblical flood of Noah, however, provides a better explanation for rapid burial and fossilization, massive fossil graveyards, and polystrate fossils.

5. What about the dinosaurs?

Kids love the dinosaurs. A dinosaur coloring book, toy, or movie is a great way to keep them occupied...for hours. But the subject of dinosaurs is more than just kid stuff; it has serious implications on the history of our world and even on faith itself. Perhaps more than anything else, the secular history of the dinosaurs suggests to the world that the Bible is outdated and irrelevant.

The age of the dinosaurs is based on the radiometric dating of rock layers in the vicinity of dinosaur fossils. Therefore, the "certain" age of dinosaurs is subject to the same weaknesses as the fossil record and scientific dating methods, an uncertain foundation to say the least (see Science Question 3 and 4).

So how does the Bible explain the dinosaurs? Here are a few key elements[53]:

- Formed: God created them on Day 6 along with the other land animals and man (Genesis 1:24-26).
- Fell: They suffered the effects of Adam's fall and the curse placed upon creation (Romans 8:20-22).
- Flood: They endured the catastrophic global flood of Noah, although one pair of each kind of dinosaur was saved aboard the Ark (Genesis 6:19-20).[54]
- Faded: After the flood, they spread out to repopulate the earth, but over time became extinct like many other animals in the harsh post-flood world.

Why doesn't the Bible use the word *dinosaur?*

- The word was not invented until 1841 by Sir Richard Owen.
- The dinosaur issue—so fascinating to us—was not an important issue to them.

6. The Genesis creation account was taken from other cultures.

Is Genesis 1-11 another story borrowed from other cultures? Let's look at two key parts of the Genesis account, creation and the flood, and analyze these claims.

The Creation. Similar stories from the Near East, like the Babylonian and Sumerian creation accounts, are said to be the basis for the Genesis story. However, these accounts don't explain creation as the act of a single, infinite God, but as a result of a battle between many limited gods. Also, per these accounts, humanity was created by mixing an evil god's blood with clay.

The Genesis account by comparison is simple and less mythological.[55] "In the Ancient Near East," notes Josh McDowell, "the rule is that simple accounts or traditions give rise (by accretion and embellishment) to elaborate legends, but not the reverse."[56]

The Flood. The Greeks, Hindus, Chinese, Mexicans, Algonquins, and Hawaiians have stories of an ancient, global flood. But, like the creation account, their renditions are less believable and more mythological in nature. Also, only Genesis gives the year of the flood and a chronology of Noah's life.

The Babylonian account contains a cube-shaped ship (which would have been very unstable in the raging seas), and other pagan accounts have the rainfall lasting only seven days and the waters subsiding in only one day.[57] "Another striking difference between Genesis and the other versions is that in these accounts the hero is granted immortality and exalted. The Bible moves on to Noah's sin. Only a version that seeks to tell the truth would include this realistic admission."[58]

7. There is no evidence of a global flood.

Here are six evidences of a global flood as presented by Answers in Genesis[59]:

1. *Fossils of sea creatures high above sea level.* Fossilized sea creatures appear in rock layers on every continent, including the Grand Canyon (over a mile above sea level) and the Himalayas.

2. *Rapid burial of plants and animals.* Graveyards of well preserved fossils exist all over the world. Billions of nautiloid fossils (squid-like creatures with a shell[60]) are found in the Redwall Limestone of the Grand Canyon. Other examples include the chalk and coal beds of Europe and the United States. The quality of the fossils is evidence of rapid burial.

3. *Rapidly deposited sediment layers spread across vast areas.* Rock layers that extend across and even between continents and physical characteristics in those strata indicate the material was laid down rapidly.

4. *Sediment transported long distances.* Some of the sediment in those widespread rock layers, like the sand from the Coconino Sandstone of the Grand Canyon, had to be eroded and carried long distances by fast moving water.

5. *Rapid or no erosion between strata.* Contrary to the teaching of evolutionary geology, no slow and gradual erosion has

been found between rock layers. In fact, the opposite has been observed: rapid erosion between strata.

6. *Many strata laid down in rapid succession.* Rocks don't normally bend, but break as they become hard and brittle. In many places, however, we find rock layers that bent without cracking or splintering showing the layers were laid down rapidly and flexed while still soft.

8. Miracles are scientifically impossible.

Many miracles require the suspension of the normal principles of nature in order to occur, but not all do. The parting of the Rea Sea was caused when "the Lord drove the sea back with a strong east wind and turned it into dry land" (Exodus 14:21). Here the timing of events and the direct cause of the wind were divinely ordered for a purpose. In this case, science can offer no criticism because the miracle was accomplished within the normal workings of nature.

However, there are miracles that come about against the laws of nature, like the Resurrection, and come under fire by the scientific community. Below is a listing and response to common criticisms:

1. *Physical laws cannot be broken.* Physical laws only describe how the universe normally operates. If there is a supernatural Creator who brought those laws into existence, what is to preclude him from suspending them for a specific reason? Nothing.

2. *No one has seen a miracle.* Of course, the Bible is a book documenting eyewitness accounts to specific miracles by God. But what most people mean here is I've never seen a miracle. By definition, miracles are rare, so it is no surprise that most of us haven't seen one. As someone has said, "I've never seen the dark side of the moon either, but that doesn't

mean it doesn't exist."

3. *There is no God.* More times than not, this is the real issue for most people. Before they even consider the evidence for miracles, they've already concluded they can't happen because there is no God to perform them. But if God is real...

9. Great scientists, like Galileo, have been persecuted by the church.

The supposed persecution of Galileo is said to demonstrate the intolerance of the Christian community to scientific progress. Interestingly, however, the facts of the case show the opposite.

In his book, *What's so great about Christianity?*, Dinesh D'Souza takes up the issue and gives a rarely heard historical account.[61] Here is a summary of his findings:

- The issue of whether the earth revolved around the sun or the sun revolved around the earth (heliocentricity or geocentricity) was not settled at the time.
- The pope admired and supported Galileo, as did the head of the Inquisition, Cardinal Bellarmine.
- Given the unproven nature of Galileo's theory and the serious scriptural considerations, Bellarmine issued an injunction that Galileo was not to teach or promote heliocentrism, to which Galileo agreed.
- Later Galileo renewed his public teaching and promotion of heliocentrism and published a book supporting it.
- In his book, Galileo made several critical mistakes: 1) his proofs were wrong, 2) he embarrassed the pope by

creating a simpleton character obviously intended to represent the pope, and 3) he taught that the Bible was mostly allegorical and must be continually reinterpreted.

- In the end, he was not found guilty of heresy, but of failing to keep his agreement with Bellarmine and was sentenced to house arrest.
- Galileo was never placed in a dungeon or tortured in any way.

Chapter 12
Truth Questions

Truth Questions	
1. No one has all the truth.	136
2. Truth is different for every person.	136
3. All paths lead to the same God.	137
4. What about Islam and Buddhism?	138
5. There is no absolute truth.	139
6. We should tolerate everyone's beliefs.	140
7. Shouldn't we just focus on the common truth of love in all religions?	141

1. No one has all the truth.

I had a great conversation with a woman on an airplane one day. We talked about spiritual things for an hour and covered every conceivable topic. At one point she said this, "No one has all the truth." At the time I wasn't sure exactly how to respond. But as I thought about it later, a few key things came to mind.

First, if no one has all the truth, how do you know your statement is true? Maybe it is a part of the truth that no one can know. This statement is self-refuting: if it's true, it can't be true.

Second, although this nice lady was certain I didn't have all the truth, she certainly held some strong views herself on most major spiritual issues. She was *certain* God was not personal or knowable. She was *certain* there was no heaven or hell. She was *certain* the Bible was not God's Word to mankind. She was *certain* Jesus was not divine and she was *certain* he was never resurrected from the dead.

For someone who didn't believe anyone can know all the truth, she sure did know a lot of the core truths of life!

The point is, we all have a core set of beliefs about life, God, and spiritual things. No one really believes "no one has all the truth"—we each believe we have it! But because we (my airplane friend and I) believe things that contradict—about the Resurrection, for example—one of us is right and one wrong. Of that we both can be certain.

2. Truth is different for every person.

What some people say is that each person creates their own truth. You have yours and I have mine. And there is no overarching truth that applies to all of us.

There is some truth to this. When it comes to the opinions or preferences of individuals (I think chocolate is the best ice cream flavor; he thinks strawberry is), yes, each person has their own truth. But, outside of a few limited situations, this view just doesn't hold up. Let me give you a few flaws in this thinking:

Many everyday examples show this statement cannot be true. "You have to eat every day. That's true for you, but not for me." "My boss says I have to be at work at eight, but that's just his truth. I have a different view."

Views that contradict cannot both be true. If your truth is that the Bible is corrupt and my view is that the Bible is not corrupt, one of us is wrong because our views contradict. If we start allowing contradictions to be true, then our entire world degrades into meaningless insanity.

You can't be sure you're right about the most important things in life. If everybody's truth about God, the afterlife, and heaven and hell is equally valid then there's no way for me to set my view apart as right or another as wrong. In the end, I can't be sure about any of the most important aspects of life. Can you really live with that?

You can't argue against evil. If everybody's truth is valid, then Hitler's is valid. But nobody really believes that.

Despite our attempts to conceal it, there is an overarching truth that applies to all of us. The Bible says our reality is built on the absolute reality of a personal, knowable God who, through his nature and Word, has defined for us what is true and what is false, what is right and what is wrong.

3. All paths lead to the same God.

If there's one thing I could encourage you to do through this book, it would be to learn how to think critically. I don't mean be a critical person, always criticizing others, but to discern good thinking from bad, logical arguments from illogical ones.

This is one of those illogical ones.

Let's say you want to go from Raleigh, NC, to Washington, DC, so you ask two people for directions. One guy says to take I-95 north and another guy says take I-95 south. Now, just in case you're not familiar with the geography of the East Coast, if you follow I-95 south from Raleigh, you'll end up in Miami! You've got to go north to make it to DC. Both of these directions can't be right—lead you to the same place—because they contradict each other. And a contradiction can never be true.

In a similar way, when we say that all paths lead to the same God, we're saying a contradiction can be true. When you analyze the core teachings of the world's religions, you find they continually contradict each other.

For example, Christianity claims Jesus Christ was physically resurrected from the dead. Islam says the opposite. Because these contradict, one has to be right and the other wrong, but both cannot be true. The real problem here—one you've got to get over—is not wanting to believe that some people are right and some are wrong. It doesn't mean they're stupid, or should be hated or oppressed, or that God doesn't care for them. It simply means they're wrong.

4. What about Islam and Buddhism?

Two of the world's largest religions, other than Christianity, are Islam and Buddhism. What do these teach and how are they different from Christianity?

Islam, meaning "submission," is a religion developed from the teachings of Muhammad, an Arab born in Mecca in A.D. 570. It has two major schools, Sunnite, by far the largest, and Shi'ite. Islam teaches a single god, but not a Trinity, rejects the Bible as a source of reliable revelation from God, denies Jesus is the Son of God, and declares salvation can be found only by accomplishing the Five Pillars of the Faith.[62]

Buddhism was developed from Siddhartha Gautama, a rich nobleman of the fifth century B.C. Buddhists seek to escape the cycles of rebirth by experiencing Nirvana, a state without suffering. Nirvana is accomplished by following the Eightfold path: Right belief, resolve, word, act, life, effort, thinking, and meditation. There is no personal God in Buddhism, and, of course, no personal Savior.[63]

In terms of deciding which is true, I turn you back to the law of contradiction. The major teachings of each religion contradict the major teachings of Christianity (nature of God, method of salvation, nature and role of Jesus Christ, the Bible). Therefore, on the issues in question, one must be wrong and one right. For example, Buddhism says God is not personal; Christianity says he is. One is right and the other is wrong.

5. There is no absolute truth.

Let me give you three weaknesses of believing this statement.

1. *It is self-refuting.* This statement is itself an absolute statement. When you say it, you are presenting it as truth, making the claim invalid in the process. Here are few other statements that do this:

- "No one can know the truth." So how can you know what you just said is true?
- "You can't know you're right and others are wrong." And how do you *know* that?

- "We shouldn't judge others." But isn't *that* a judgment?

2. *It is unlivable.* Another major problem is that you can't be consistent with this view in real life. When someone says they don't believe in absolutes, ask them if they believe genocide is ever right. "Of course not," they'll reply.

3. *It undermines my ability to know anything.* In spite of the self-refuting nature of this claim, if I insist on holding to it anyway (which many do), I am accepting a contradiction as part of my worldview. When I do that, I can never actually know anything, because then any claim made by anyone can mean absolutely anything, no matter how absurd.[64]

The bottom line is that we all hold absolute beliefs in some respect for moral and spiritual things. We just differ on which truths we want to believe. So how do we decide between opposing views? There must be an absolute standard by which we can measure our beliefs. The Bible gives us that standard, the Word of the eternal, foundation of all existence, God.

6. We should tolerate everyone's beliefs.

It depends on what you mean by this. If you mean we should allow others to believe what they want without fear of mistreatment or oppression, yes.

However, if you mean I must allow others to do whatever they want regardless of the costs to individual human beings and society overall, no. If tolerance means I have to say everyone is right, give up my freedom to call someone out for promoting lies, and cease all efforts to show others the light of the Bible and Jesus of Nazareth, no. If tolerance means I have to allow false teachings to spread about the Bible, God, and Christianity, watch quietly as others rewrite history and lay the intellectual foundation to take away my rights, no.

I'm afraid this is what most people mean when they talk about tolerance. These are not the words they use, but this is what they say by their actions. What it really means is that I, as a Christian, must tolerate everybody else's views—no matter how crude or offensive—and keep my mouth shut. All the while people from every angle criticize, mock, and labor to destroy everything I believe in and hold dear.

If you are a non-Christian, I ask you to step back and listen as if you were. Count how many times the name Jesus is used as an expletive on television each night. Hear as the Bible is taunted and attacked by a constant procession of supposed "historical" or "scientific" television shows. Notice how my faith is chiseled off monuments and shoved out of classrooms. Then you tell me, who's really the intolerant lot in America?

7. Shouldn't we just focus on the common truth of love in all religions?

In the first place, I'm not so sure there is a common truth of love in all religions. Atheism's core teaching (atheism is a religion that worships man) is survival of the fittest. Any attempt to promote love must come from outside the belief system itself.

Hinduism teaches that one's pitiful circumstances are a result of karma and are therefore divinely appointed (hence the Caste system). Islam, while many argue is a religion of love, produces inhumane treatment of women, holy war against unbelievers, and grievous violations of human rights (for links to articles on violence in Islam, see www.thereligionofpeace.com).

Whatever common urge we share toward love comes from

three possible sources. In the first place, we are made in the image of God (Genesis 1:26) and have each been given a conscience (Romans 2:14-15). Furthermore, western cultures have all been heavily influenced by Jesus Christ and the Bible. Finally, it is politically correct to "love," promote acts of mercy, and show oneself to be generous.

Even if a common code of love can be identified, does that answer life's ultimate questions? Let's say we all agree on what love is and how to practice it, and then we all labor to demonstrate love as we have agreed. How does that answer the question, Why is there suffering in our world? Why do people die? What comes after death? Who is God and how can I please him (or it)?

It doesn't. We search for God because we need more than a common definition of love; we need someone to explain this life to us, and offer us a way out of it. If you want to focus on something, focus on this element of religion. When you do, you'll find that the Bible alone satisfies the great questions of life.

Chapter 13

Church & Christianity Questions

Church and Christianity Questions	
1. "Christians" do as much evil as anybody else.	144
2. What about the Crusades?	144
3. Why are Christians always asking for money?	146
4. You don't have to go to church to be a good person.	147
5. The true meaning of Christianity is found in hidden meaning, symbols, and sects.	148
6. Christianity developed from other religions and their teachings.	149
7. Why are there so many churches and denominations?	150
8. Why are some groups called "cults"?	151
9. I'm not into "organized religion."	152

1. "Christians" do as much evil as anybody else.

Many misunderstand what it means to be a real Christian. It doesn't mean we become perfect and never sin again. It means we have repented of our sins, trusted in the sacrifice of Jesus as payment for our sins, and now vow to live for Christ until we die. However, we retain our sin nature and war with it for the rest of our lives.

Furthermore, much of the evil done in the name of Christ in the past was not done by genuine Christians, but by governments falsely flying the Christian flag. This is nothing new and is not unique to Christianity.[65]

"Religious" people—religious *hypocrites* to be more accurate—have always plagued the earth. Even during the time of Jesus, they were a thorn in humanity's side. Jesus reserved his harshest words for the "scribes and Pharisees." But then, as now, those on the outside could tell the difference.

Also realize you live in a culture blessed by the benevolent, sacrificial work of genuine Christians. "Almost every one of the first 123 colleges and universities in the United States has Christian origins."[66] Furthermore, in America "the first hospitals were started largely by Christians."

Think of the names, Baptist Hospital, Methodist Hospital, St Luke's Presbyterian.[67] And don't forget the Salvation Army, Red Cross, and YMCA (Young Men's Christian Association), among others.

2. What about the Crusades?

Since the time Jesus walked the earth, several notable crimes have been committed in his name. One of the most famous is the Crusades launched by the Roman Catholic church in 1095 in an attempt to regain control of the Holy

Land from Muslim rule. Time does not permit a full discussion of the subject, so let me give you a few points to consider regarding this issue:

- The Roman Catholic Church did not at that time and does not now represent biblical Christianity. In the view of many conservative, biblical Christians, the Catholic Church left its biblical roots long before the Crusades with teachings like purgatory, indulgences, sainthood, confession, and papal infallibility.
- Carrying out acts of war and forced conversion is absolutely forbidden by the teachings of Christ and the apostles and represents true sin by those who claim the name of Christ, whether Protestant or Catholic.
- The Crusades demonstrate the danger of establishing a religious state. Nowhere in the New Testament is it taught or implied that true Christians should establish and control secular government. There's a good reason for this.
- Not all who claimed to be "Christian" were the real thing. "In times past Christendom was comprised of people living in 'Christian' territories."[69] Many of the rulers of so-called "Christian" nations, as well as many people living within their borders, we no more Christian than the Muslims they fought.
- True Christians also sin, and some took part in the darkest acts in church history like the Crusades. The Christian continues to struggle with his sinful nature until death, and sometimes that nature produces terrible actions.

3. Why are Christians always asking for money?

"It's just a racket." That's the attitude of many people when it comes to Christian churches and ministries. And it's hard to argue with them when you see men in thousand dollar suits on television asking the struggling single mother to "sow a seed" into their ministry, and women flying around in private jets promising health and wealth if you'll just "send us a check." It's disgusting.

So, is all Christian work only a front for lining one's pockets? I can tell you from personal experience, no!

First, there probably wouldn't be any charities if it wasn't for Jesus and his followers. "One scholar, Dr. Martineau, exhaustively searched through historical documents and concluded that antiquity has left no trace of any organized charitable effort.... When Christ and the Bible became known, charity and benevolence flourished."[70]

Second, though the heart of the genuine Christ-follower is to do ministry for free, there are real costs that cannot be overlooked. Ministries hire staff and those staff members have kids and mortgages to pay. Ministries have insurance costs and printing and rent. They must have financial help or they will cease to exist. Because of this, ministry leaders are forced to ask for help. If you don't ask, people don't give.

Finally, I've seen the sacrifices ministry leaders and staff make to keep their work going. Just recently, I met a CEO of a large Christian ministry at a conference in Chicago. He looked tired, so I asked him if he slept well. He told me he had slept on the floor of an empty house so the ministry wouldn't have to pay for a hotel.

Instead of judging those who ask for your help, open

your wallet and feel the joy of giving to organizations who are genuinely trying to help the community and the world.

4. You don't have to go to church to be a good person.

This statement is due to a misunderstanding of 1) why Christians go to church and 2) what it takes to be right with God.

Church. Christians don't go to church because they think it will make them better than everybody else, because it's the only way to foster moral improvement, or because it makes them right with God. Christians meet with other Christians each week to worship Jesus Christ, experience the love of brothers and sisters, and be transformed by learning the Word of God.

Right with God. We all know that some level of goodness is required to be accepted by our Maker. In our culture, we all believe we've attained that level of goodness. We look around at everybody else and say, "I'm not that bad." But God doesn't compare us to each other to determine our goodness—he compares us to himself.

To be right with God, you must be morally perfect, without a single strike on your record. If you commit five sins a day (which is pretty good) and live seventy years, you'll have more than 100,000 sins to account for on Judgment Day. Because of this, each of us is on the wrong side of an eternal, righteous, all-powerful God who has declared us all guilty.

There's only one escape, but it's freely available to all. Repent of your sins, trust that Jesus Christ died in your place, and commit to live the rest of your life to serve him. When you do this, your debt is wiped away and you are right with God forever.

5. The true meaning of Christianity is found in hidden meanings, symbols, and sects.

Our culture is obsessed with what may be hidden, locked away, or kept secret. Consequently, we discount anything that comes from the past as suspect, a bold attempt by the powers-that-be to control and manipulate us. From Dan Brown's novels, to the *National Treasure* movies, to groups seeking meaning in hidden patterns of biblical numbers—the evidence of our paranoia is all around us. Where will it end?

The cause of this fear is not increasing evidence that the truth has been hidden from us, but that our culture has lost something foundational—we've lost trust. We've lost trust in our fellow man because he has grown more and more untrustworthy. He swindles us; he deceives us; he lies.

We've lost our trust in God. We're not sure who he is anymore. Some people say he's not even there, others say he's not involved, others say he's a mindless presence in us all. We don't know him anymore, so we don't know how to trust him.

This lack of trust of both God and man can ultimately be traced back to our rejection of the Bible. As we have freed ourselves of its moral wisdom, we have lost our integrity and trustworthiness; as we have ignored the clear portrait of the God it reveals, we have lost the rock and anchor of our lives.

In spite of what you fear, the true meaning of Christianity is not hidden from you. Open its pages and read for yourself. The God of light, who wrote it, has designed it for all to understand.

6. Christianity developed from other religions and their teachings.

While it makes for a good story, Christianity was not developed by taking bits and pieces of other religions and myths and creating the Jesus narrative. In general, attempts to do this make the following errors:

- Assume the Bible is wrong with very little research into the questions raised.
- Take for granted that the biblical authors were liars, in spite of their clear teaching to the contrary.
- Assume the evolution of history and the "god concept."
- Assume that if any similarities exist, Christianity must have borrowed from that source.
- Ignore glaring dissimilarities between accounts.

Here are a few biblical elements that are often accused of being borrowed:[71]

- The Genesis creation account. Other accounts describe creation as the result of a battle between limited gods, and man's creation by mixing clay with the blood of an evil god.
- The Genesis flood. Only Genesis gives dates, chronology, and a realistic account of the hero.
- The Ten Commandments. Egyptian *Book of the Dead* (BOD) has forty-two commands whereas Genesis has only ten. The BOD has forty-two gods whereas Genesis has only one.
- The life of Jesus. As an example, Asclepius, Greek god of healing, a supposed source for Jesus' life, was born of

a sexual relationship between his human mother and Apollo, was pulled from his mother's womb on a funeral pyre, and was given to a centaur named Chiron who became his tutor.

7. Why are there so many churches and denominations?

Presbyterian, Baptist, Methodist, Lutheran, Pentecostal, Nondenominational. It's confusing, isn't it? So why all the differences and what does it mean to me? There are several reasons different denominations exist. Let me list and explain a few:

- *Different practices:* In some churches, the minister wears a robe; in others, a suit; still others, a Hawaiian shirt. Some churches use a band, others a choir, others no music at all.
- *Different teachings:* Some teach baptism by immersion and others by sprinkling. Some believe sign gifts are still active, others believe they have ceased. Some hold to independent churches while others teach a hierarchical form of church government.
- *Conflict:* As I said earlier, Christians are sinners too. Sometimes folks just get mad and set out on their own. God hates conflict, but he turns it for good.

As someone considering a life of following Jesus Christ (at least, I hope you are), what recommendations do I have for you regarding visiting or joining a church?

1. The church must believe and teach the Christian Bible as their sole authority.[72] This precludes cults like Mormons, Jehovah's Witnesses, and others, as well as the Catholic Church.

2. The church must believe that Jesus is the lone instrument for salvation from sin. No church that believes in multiple paths to God or salvation through any type of good works should be considered.

3. The church must teach and practice strong biblical morality. The church should preach moral change—not perfection—as an absolute requirement of genuine Christianity.

8. Why are some groups called "cults"?

In Walter Martin's famous book, *Kingdom of the Cults*, he defines a cult as "a group of people gathered about a specific person or person's *misinterpretation* of the Bible"[73] [emphasis original]. The term, though it has a negative connotation in the culture, is not intended to be disrespectful or insulting.

Cults have several important characteristics. First, they appeal to an authority other than the Bible itself. The Mormon's have Joseph Smith's *Book of Mormon*; Christian Scientists have Mary Baker Eddy's *Science and Health with Key to the Scriptures*.[74] Second, they use Scripture frequently but almost always out of context. Finally, they change the meaning of common Christian terms but use them as if they had not.

So what's the problem? Don't they have the right to believe whatever they want? Of course, they do. But you have the right to know what they believe and the results of following in their spiritual footsteps. The central problem is this: If the Bible, understood in its original context as intended by its original authors, is the truth from God about himself, heaven and hell, salvation, and righteous living, then any deviation from that—and modern cults deviate greatly—jeopardizes not only your ability to live right in the sight of God, but also your eternal destiny.

Inasmuch as cults misrepresent the true teachings of Scripture, they turn their adherents from the life of God in every sense.

9. I'm not in to "organized religion."

It is popular today to be "spiritual" but not "religious," to have beliefs, pray, contemplate the divine, and practice spiritual rituals, but not go to a house of worship or join a religious group or church. Some teachers even encourage this. "The new spirituality…is arising to a large extent outside of the structures of the existing institutionalized religions."[75]

There are many reasons for this trend. Some have been hurt by religious people. Some don't want their weekend schedule interrupted. Some want to avoid conflict, and others just want to avoid accountability for their lifestyle.

The thought behind this trend is good. People are realizing that our connection with God does not come through a person or group. But is the trend itself good? To determine this I suggest we ask God what he wants. Is it God's will that I avoid gathered groups of believers?

When you become convinced that the Bible is God's communication to man (which I've tried to demonstrate in this book), you stop turning to pundits and preachers for answers and instead seek guidance from the Bible itself.

The Bible states clearly that it is God's will for his people to gather on a regular basis (Hebrews 10:25). Church is not the building; it is the people. And God desires his people to gather in order to a) worship him, b) encourage and support each other, c) form a barrier of protection (accountability), d) learn his word, e) serve him, and f) pray.

The difficulties that arise out of these gatherings are also part of God's will for us.

So first I ask you to consider the claims of Christ and the Bible where salvation is concerned. And then, once you have committed your life to him, ignore the wisdom of the day and participate regularly in the gatherings of God's people.

Notes

[1] Geoffrey W. Bromiley, editor, *Theological Dictionary of the New Testament*, Abridged Edition (Grand Rapids: Eerdmans, 1985), 918.

[2] Pornography. (n.d.). Dictionary.com Unabridged (v 1.1). Accessed June 01, 2009, from Dictionary.com website: http://dictionary.classic.reference.com/browse/pornography.

[3] H. Buis, "Hell," in *Zondervan Pictorial Encyclopedia of the Bible*, Volume 3, Merrill C. Tenney, ed. (Grand Rapids: Zondervan, 1976), 115.

[4] Ibid.

[5] *Strong's Greek Lexicon in Online Bible Edition*, Version 1.42 (Ontario: Online Bible Foundation, 2004).

[6] Starting assumptions are also called presuppositions. This entire concept comes from Ken Ham at Answers in Genesis, www.answersingenesis.org.

[7] Peter Galling, "Do Creationists Reject Science?" February 4, 2008, available from www.answersingenesis.org/articles/2008/02/04/do-creationists-reject-science; internet; ac-

cessed February 7, 2008.

[8] Norman Geisler and William Watkins, *Worlds Apart: A Handbook on Worldviews* (Grand Rapids: Baker, 1989) on *The Norman L. Geisler Apologetics Library on CD-ROM* (Grand Rapids: Baker, 2002).

[9] Dictionary.com. Accessed June 24, 2010.

[10] *1689 London Baptist Confession*. "Chapter 2: Of God and the Holy Trinity," available at: www.vor.org/truth/1689; internet; accessed March 30, 2010.

[11] Jason Lisle, *The Ultimate Proof of Creation* (Green Forest, AK: Master, 2009), 38-43.

[12] Lee Strobel, *The Case for Christ* (Grand Rapids: Zondervan, 1998), 138.

[13] Josh McDowell, *The New Evidence that Demands a Verdict* (Nashville: Thomas Nelson, 1999), 94.

[14] Ibid, 34.

[15] Ibid, 34.

[16] Randall Price, T*he Stones Cry Out: What Archaeology Reveals About the Truth of the Bible* (Eugene, Oregon: Harvest House, 1997), 278.

[17] Donald H. Madvig, "Joshua," *The Expositor's Bible Commentary, Volume 3*, Frank E. Gaebelein, General Editor (Zondervan: Grand Rapids, 1992), 247. Each point in this section comes from this source.

[18] A. Rupprecht, "Slavery," in *The Zondervan Pictorial Encyclopedia of the Bible*, Volume 5, Merrill C. Tenney, General Editor (Grand Rapids: Zondervan, 1976), 456.

[19] James S. Jeffers, *The Greco-Roman World of the New Testament Era* (Downers Grove, IL: InterVarsity Press, 1999), 222.

[20] Erwin Lutzer, *The DaVinci Deception* (Carol Stream, IL:

2006), 92.

[21] Ibid, 96.

[22] "Gnostic, Gnostic Gospels, and Gnosticism," available from http://www.earlychristianwritings.com/gnostics.html; Internet; accessed August 29, 2008.

[23] *The Book of the Dead*, "Chapter 125: The Judgment of the Dead," available at http://www.wsu.edu/~dee/EGYPT/BOD125.HTM; internet; accessed May 11, 2010.

[24] The points and quotations listed here taken from McDowell, 120-123.

[25] Strobel, 212.

[26] Ibid, 183.

[27] "Bible translations," available at: http://en.wikipedia.org/wiki/Bible_translations; internet; accessed April 27, 2010.

[28] Lee Strobel quoting J. P. Moreland in *The Case for Christ* (Grand Rapids: Zondervan, 1998), 333.

[29] "Original or a copy?" available at http://www.bandoli.no/nooriginaljesus.htm; internet; accessed April 27, 2010.

[30] Ron Leadbetter, "Asclepius," available at http://www.pantheon.org/articles/a/asclepius.html; internet; accessed April 27, 2010.

[31] Eckhart Tolle, *The Power of Now* (Novato, CA: Namaste Publishing and New World Library, 1999), 104.

[32] Ibid.

[33] Ibid.

[34] Ibid.

[35] Ibid, 38, 64, and 143.

[36] Ibid, 104.

[37] Eckhart Tolle, *A New Earth* (New York, NY: Penguin Group2005), 1-5 and 14-15.

[38] This is the number at the time of this writing, July 2010.

[39] Patterson, 45.

[40] Ibid.

[41] Lisle, *The New Answers Book 2*, 107.

[42] Patterson, 50.

[43] For further study, visit www.creation.com or www.answersingenesis.org.

[44] All data in this section was taken from Lane Lester, "Genetics: no friend of evolution, A highly qualified biologist tells it like it is," Creation Magazine, March 1998, 20-22.

[45] Roger Patterson, *Evolution Exposed: Biology* (Hebron, KY: Answers in Genesis, 2007), 58.

[46] Don Batten, ed., *The Revised and Expanded Answers Book* (Green Forest, AK: Master Books, 2003), 83-86.

[47] Ibid.

[48] For a thorough study of the dating methods issue, visit http://www.answersingenesis.org/get-answers/topic/radiometric-dating.

[49] Andrew Snelling, "Doesn't the Order of the Fossils in the Rock Record Favor Long Ages?" in *The New Answers Book 2*, Ken Ham, general editor (Green Forest, AK: 2008), 342.

[50] Patterson, *Evolution Exposed: Earth Science*, 150.

[51] Ibid.

[52] Ibid, 152.

[53] This teaching is taken from Answers in Genesis. For a detailed study visit http://www.answersingenesis.org/get-answers/topic/dinosaurs.

[54] Visit Answers in Genesis for a full discussion of Noah's Ark: http://www.answersingenesis.org/get-answers/topic/noahs-ark.

[55] McDowell, 101.

[56] Ibid.

[57] Ibid, 104-105.

[58] Ibid, 105.

[59] "Worldwide Flood, Worldwide Evidence," available at http://www.answersingenesis.org/get-answers/features/worldwide-flood-evidence; internet; accessed April 27, 2010.

[60] Patterson, *Evolution Exposed: Earth Science*, 150.

[61] Dinesh D'Souza, *What's so great about Christianity?* (Carol Stream, IL: Tyndale, 2007), 103-113. Others have labored along the same lines. I refer you to "The Galileo affair: history or heroic hagiography?" by Thomas Schirrmacher, available at: http://www.answersingenesis.org/tj/v14/i1/galileo.asp; internet; accessed April 27, 2010.

[62] Walter Martin, *The Kingdom of the Cults* (Minneapolis: Bethany House, 2003), 436-448.

[63] Ibid, 300-303.

[64] Lisle, *Ultimate Proof*, 137-138.

[65] For a full treatment of this subject and well known Christian sins, see chapter 14 of D. James Kennedy and Jerry Newcombe's book, *What if Jesus had never been born?* (Nashville: Thomas Nelson, 1994), 205-223.

[66] Ibid, 52.

[67] Ibid, 147.

[68] Ibid, 209.

[69] Ibid.

[70] Ibid, 29.

[71] These have been addressed separately as Science Question 6 and 7, Bible Question 7, and Jesus Question 6.

[72] This would include belief in one God, the Trinity, Jesus' divinity, and other historic, conservative Christian teachings.

[73] Martin, 18. I recommend this work for an in-depth study of this entire subject.

[74] Ibid, 38.

[75] Tolle, *A New Earth*, 19.

Appendix 1
Recommended Resources

Here are some resources I recommend for further study. Most of these resources are available at Evidence America's Online Superstore at www.evidenceamerica.org.

Evangelism:

- *Evangelism Starter Kit*, low-cost kit including evangelism training books, DVDs, and witnessing booklets, available at www.evidenceamerica.org.
- *Forcefully Advancing: The Last Hope for America and American Christianity*, Wes Moore, available at www.evidenceamerica.org.
- *Forcefully Advancing Video Curriculum*, 7-part DVD series based on the book, produced by Evidence America, available at www.evidenceamerica.org.
- *The Maker*, Wes Moore, apologetics/evangelism novel designed to convert the lost, Provectus Media, 2010, available at www.evidenceamerica.org.

General Questions and Answers (DVD):

- *Apologetics Starter Kit*, low-cost kit including apologetics books on various subjects and apologetics DVDs, available at www.evidenceamerica.org.
- *Respond Apologetics Course*, DVD curriculum, produced by Evidence America, www.evidenceamerica.org.
- *Respond Apologetics Course*, online version, www.apologeticscurriculum.com.

General Questions and Answer (Book):

- *Apologetics Starter Kit*, low-cost kit including apologetics books on various subjects and apologetics DVDs, available at www.evidenceamerica.org.
- *The Maker,* Wes Moore, apologetics/evangelism novel designed to convert the lost, Provectus Media, 2010, available at www.evidenceamerica.org.
- *Evidence for Christianity*, Josh McDowell, Thomas Nelson, 2006.
- *The New Evidence that Demands a Verdict*, Josh McDowell, Thomas Nelson, 1999.
- *The Evidence Bible,* Ray Comfort, Bridge-logos, 2003.

God Questions:

- *Apologetics Starter Kit*, low-cost kit including apologetics books on various subjects and apologetics DVDs, available at www.evidenceamerica.org.
- *Evidence for Christianity,* Josh McDowell, Thomas Nelson, 2006.
- *Is there really a God?* Booklet, Ken Ham.
- *The Maker*, Wes Moore, apologetics/evangelism novel designed to convert the lost, Provectus Media, 2010, available at www.evidenceamerica.org.

- *The New Evidence that Demands a Verdict*, Josh McDowell, Thomas Nelson, 1999.
- *When Skeptics Ask: A Handbook on Christian Evidences*, Norman Geisler and Norman Brooks, Baker Books, 2008.

Bible Questions:

- *Apologetics Starter Kit*, low-cost kit including apologetics books on various subjects and apologetics DVDs, available at www.evidenceamerica.org.
- *Making Sense of Bible Difficulties*, Norman Geisler, Baker Books, 2009.
- *Searching for the Original Bible*, Randall Price.
- *The Case for Christ*, Lee Strobel, Zondervan, 1998.
- *When Skeptics Ask: A Handbook on Christian Evidences*, Norman Geisler and Norman Brooks, Baker Books, 2008.

Jesus Questions:

- *Apologetics Starter Kit*, low-cost kit including apologetics books on various subjects and apologetics DVDs, available at www.evidenceamerica.org.
- *Evidence for the Resurrection*, Josh and Sean McDowell, Gospel Light, 2009.
- *The Case for Christ*, Lee Strobel, Zondervan, 1998.
- *The Case for the Real Jesus*, Lee Strobel, Zondervan, 2007.

Science and Evolution:

- *Apologetics Starter Kit*, low-cost kit including apologetics books on various subjects and apologetics DVDs, available at www.evidenceamerica.org.

- *The Maker*, Wes Moore, apologetics/evangelism novel designed to convert the lost, Provectus Media, 2010, available at www.evidenceamerica.org.
- *The New Answers Book*, Ken Ham, editor, Master Books, 2006.
- *The New Answers Book 2*, Ken Ham, editor, Master Books, 2008.
- *The New Answers Book 3*, Ken Ham, editor, Master Books, 2008.
- *Refuting Evolution*, Jonathan Sarfati, Master Books, 1999.
- *The Stones Cry Out*, Randall Price, Harvest House, 1997.

Truth Questions:

- *Apologetics Starter Kit*, low-cost kit including apologetics books on various subjects and apologetics DVDs, available at www.evidenceamerica.org.
- *The New Evidence that Demands a Verdict*, Josh McDowell, Thomas Nelson, 1999.
- *They All Can't Be Right: Do all paths lead to God?* Steve Russo, B&H Publishing, 2004.

Christianity vs. Other Faith Systems:

- *Apologetics Starter Kit*, low-cost kit including apologetics books on various subjects and apologetics DVDs, available at www.evidenceamerica.org.
- *Fast Facts on False Teachings*, Ron Carlson, Harvest House, 2003.
- *Reasoning from the Scriptures with Catholics*, Ron Rhodes, Harvest House, 2000.
- *Reasoning from the Scriptures with Mormons*, Ron

Rhodes, Harvest House, 1995.

- *Reasoning from the Scriptures with Muslims,* Ron Rhodes, Harvest House, 2002.
- *The Kingdom of the Cults,* Walter Martin, Bethany Books, 2003.
- *They All Can't Be Right: Do all paths lead to God?* Steve Russo, B&H Publishing, 2004.
- *World Religions in a Nutshell,* Ray Comfort, Bridge-Logos, 2008.

Web Sites:

- Evidence America, www.evidenceamerica.org.
- The Maker Novel, www.themakernovel.com.
- Forcefully Advancing, www.forcefullyadvancingthebook.com.
- Answers in Genesis, www.answersingenesis.org.
- Norman Geisler, www.normangeisler.net.
- Gary Habermas, www.garyhabermas.com.
- Erwin Lutzer, www.moodychurch.org/radio.
- Ravi Zacharias, www.rzim.org.
- Lee Strobel, www.leestrobel.com.
- Randall Price, www.worldofthebible.com.

Learn answers to faith questions
DVD or online course

by Wes Moore
www.evidenceamerica.org

It's 300 years in the future.
America has been destroyed...
and all history of her erased.
The Global Government's power
cannot be challenged.
Until Adrien Bach digs up
the greatest crime in human history.
Their crime.
THE MAKER
a novel by
wes moore

CPSIA information can be obtained at www.ICGtesting.com
Printed in the USA
LVOW111411290312

275304LV00003B/162/P